A SOCCER PIONEER

The Autobiography of Gordon Jago

with Wayne Barton

To Robin
Thank you for your friendship
Best Wishes
Gordon

SJP
ST. JOHANN PRESS
Haworth, New Jersey

ST. JOHANN PRESS

Published in the United States of America
by St. Johann Press
P.O. Box 241
Haworth, NJ 07641
www.stjohannpress.com

The paper used in this publication meets the minimum requirements of the American National Standard for Information Sciences—Permanence of Paper for Printed Library Materials, ANSI/NISO Z39/48-1992

Proceeds from the sale of this book are being donated to the June Jago Memorial Fund in support of the Dallas Fallen Officer Foundation.

Composition and interior design by Susan Ramundo (susan@srdesktopservices.com)
Cover design, printing and binding by G&H SOHO, Inc. (www.ghsoho.com)

ISBN 978-1-937943-39-4

Manufactured in the United States of America

To June and Kim for a wonderful life

Contents

Introduction

ENJOYMENT OF PROFESSION

"If you wish to have a large house, with a big swimming pool, a Mercedes in the garage, an Armani suit and money in the bank, then go for it."

THESE WERE THE first words of advice that I gave to the Texas A&M University Sports Marketing graduating students when asked to address the group on their graduation into the wide world of earning a living. Twenty-seven young men and four young women all between the ages of 22 to 25 were in attendance.

There was a smile on many of the faces at my opening comment, evidence of their possible thinking.

My second piece of advice to them was that from my long experience they should give much thought to what type of environment and the type of work that they would do once they departed from the warm friendly atmosphere of Texas A&M University that they had experienced for the past four to five years.

To me an enjoyment of your profession is an absolute priority. The mentality that one has when going to work each day is so important.

I told these youngsters the story of my father, an engineer, who had spent fifty years with one engineering company. He had grown up during the First World War, experienced the Depression of the late thirties and had been exempt from military services during World War II due to his job manufacturing brass, which was needed to produce shells and bullets for the armed services. From the age of fifteen until sixty five, he worked there. His fifty-year present from the company was a gold watch and then he entered retirement. He had not looked forward to going to work each day and could not wait until Friday evening knowing that he would have two days at home with his family.

He lived until the age of 79, enjoying those last fourteen years when he did not have to get up each morning at 6 am to go to work. He could please himself with what he did each day and he took the opportunity along with my mother, with the financial aid of my sister and myself to enjoy both international and UK travel. Fourteen years of enjoyment against 50 years of unhappiness, toil and perhaps (I never could really tell) disappointment. To me this is a terrible ratio of the years of one's life.

So, why did he not change his job when he was younger? He married at a young age, had a family when my sister and I came along, a house and a mortgage. Jobs were hard to find during those years of depression, and perhaps he realized how fortunate he was to have one. Perhaps that sense stayed with him for the rest of his days. The story was at that time that there was always a line outside the factory gates of men looking for work. It is easy to say take the risk and find another job, it is another to take such action.

"Whom of you are married?" was my next question to these young men and women.

Three hands went up.

As the vast majority were single, my advice was that if their first job did not give them the enjoyment of going to work each day, finding their role interesting, perhaps even challenging and a certain satisfaction in what they were achieving then they should look for another position. They only had themselves to consider, no responsibilities so try something new.

If the second selection was not right then move again but if you continue not to find satisfaction then you must look to yourself.

What were you looking for?

Perhaps too much or for something beyond your abilities? Be honest with yourself, but again do not lose that desire to make every effort to find enjoyment in your job. Some risks are worth taking if you do so at a time when you can afford to.

I consider myself very fortunate. I had obtained an engineering degree from college and I had worked as a telecommunications engineer but the opportunity to become a professional footballer/soccer player gave me the life that I desired. It was a risk to give up a settled position not knowing if I would make the grade as a First Division player but I was single, I had no major responsibilities. If I failed then I could move on.

I have been so fortunate as a consequence. I have enjoyed a wonderful life. I have traveled the world at someone else's expense, met royalty, presidents, sports and entertainment celebrities and many other good people, but most importantly I have had so much joy in my chosen profession.

I wished them all well and I hoped that they make the right decisions for themselves in the years ahead. My life has been an incredible journey, and, more importantly, one of enjoyment of my profession.

one

War Child

MY EARLIEST MEMORIES are of standing in a bomb shelter at the end of our garden, watching bombs from German planes rain down on the capital.

I was born in Poplar, East London, but was raised on a Council Estate in Dagenham. In spite of the Blitz, because of Dad's job, we had to move *in* to London, so we moved to Plaistow, which is near West Ham United Football Club—being near their Boleyn Ground seemed exciting for me at the time, having been raised a Hammers fan. Dad would take me with five or six of his workmates and their children to their games.

Our home was not far from the London Docks. One evening, the Germans dropped what seemed like millions of incendiary bombs over the city. London was set alight, and standing at the edge of the garden, Dad held me as we observed the strange red glow which illuminated the landscape as far as we could see. Though we had a house, we really lived in the shelter. They were fairly comfortable—we had some electricity, some heat. Maybe, because I was so young, it made it easier—these things that were beyond comprehension were, in actual fact, much too difficult for a child as young as I was *to* comprehend, so in the main there was an obliviousness that I have to be thankful for. The searchlights, the gunfire, the explosions, the sound of the German planes . . . I can't say that it was fun, of course I knew that it wasn't, but I was too young for these memories to plague me as the traumatic experiences that they undoubtedly became for others.

The pressure of war was not on the kids, it was on the parents, but of course you only understand this properly when you're older. I didn't realize it was a matter of life and death. If you saw a German plane being hit, then you would hear everyone in the bomb shelters down your row start to cheer, and you of course would join in. When a British plane was hit, there was a silence, an eerie silence. It was a pause, to see if you could see the parachute, and if you knew the pilot had made it out, then of course another cheer went up. The memories are still tremendously vivid but the impact of them were not as strong as they might have been, mercifully.

Going to school was a difficult experience, however, the part of our life where the reality really hit. Our school was three stories high, with a bomb shelter underneath in case of raids during the day. There were plenty of daylight raids in the beginning of the war.

Each kid was given a little red "Oxo" gravy box which we put our name on and it contained a pack of raisins, biscuits, and some Cadbury's chocolate. The idea was that if we were bombed, then we had some food if we were trapped, and at a time when food was rationed, we never saw chocolate. There was a scene in the 1987 film "Hope and Glory" which was about the Blitz and I can't help but feel that somebody involved in telling that story must have gone to the same school as I did—one morning, when we went to school, we discovered that it had been hit and destroyed.

Rubble, everywhere.

So, as young children, what's our immediate thought?

The chocolate!

There were four or five of us, right into the rubble, scavenging for the boxes, regardless of whose name was on it. No sooner had we got in there than we heard loud police whistles and then the sound of the police telling us to get out. Of course, we were a danger to ourselves, what was remaining of the school could easily have collapsed on us, we could have got trapped under the rubble ourselves.

After that, we had to go to school in a church. Because there was obviously not nearly enough room to house all of the children at once, you would tend to only go in the morning or afternoon.

Sometimes, you'd come into school and the seat next to you would be empty. You quickly came to understand that they wouldn't be coming back. A casualty of a bombing raid.

My father told me years afterward that he had a premonition. He was worried about getting bombed, really worried. Someone from his factory had transferred from Welling in Kent to Wales and he had told Dad that we could have his house for the duration of the War and so we moved. We were there two weeks when we learned there was a direct hit on our houses back in Plaistow. Our neighbors had been in their bomb shelters but were all killed. We went back to visit relatives in the area a couple of months later and where our house once was, now stood an auxiliary water tank.

Now in Kent, or as we thought, "the countryside," having thought we'd at least "escaped" the Blitz, we instead had moved right into prime position to be struck by doodlebugs, which was what the V1 flying bombs were called. We were in the direct line. You would see them coming and if they were above you, you could almost breathe a sigh of relief (if, indeed, that is the appropriate term) because you knew it would glide and it would move further inland, as horrid as that thought was. But if the jet engine cut out before they reached your area then there was panic, a worry that there was about to be an immediate impact, and a scramble to get into the shelters ensued.

Being the grand old age I am, there are not many of us with these stories to tell, and fewer still in the United States of America, where I have made my home in later life. And isn't it strange how, as time passes and we grow older, these stories told in the developed voice but seen and experienced, nonetheless, through the eyes and ears of a child, maintain some of that nostalgia, as if to somewhat dilute the horror of it all.

When I decided to write my autobiography I had wonderful input from my good friends, many who had their own suggestions as to how it should begin, which stories I should tell, and so on and so forth. It is obvious, however, that with such longevity that I have enjoyed (regardless of whether or not these stories are of interest!), in the main, it has to be told in a chronological fashion.

However it would be remiss of me not to mention one such instance. I was on a Dallas radio show with a good friend of mine with the purpose of talking about soccer but he asked what it was like growing up in the War, and I of course duly obliged with stories like the above. And the strangest thing happened. I was contacted by schools that had that part of history on their current curriculum and they invited me to visit them and to talk to their classes.

Until the September 11, 2001 attacks, the United States had never suffered an attack that could be comparable to what we experienced in the Blitz, and at least in terms of it being a longer period of time over a greater area, one can reason that the World War II logically had a prolonged, acute impact on society. We lived without windows; we'd put sheets there when our windows were blown out.

I accepted the invitations to give presentations at schools and did my own research; I put together a small video and learned facts and figures myself about the number of planes shot down and so on, so that I would be prepared, but when I got to the school, I learned that the class was of under twelve year olds. I thought that not only was what I had prepared probably a little too bleak, but, just as it did to me at the time, it would likely just go over their heads.

I showed them the video tape and instead of going through all of these numbers, I related my own stories and memories. To explain to a youngster that they were lucky to have their classmates, that during the War, they might not come back, was something that I think they could relate to.

I don't think it was too traumatic. They learned a lot, I think, and remained engaged with the stories I told. It must have gone much better than I realized because soon after, I was inundated with similar requests at other schools. I accepted about four or five, although, my real intention of going on the radio show in the first place was to promote the Dallas Sidekicks soccer team! I still tried to continue to do that on the school visits.

The children varied in age and when I was giving the talk to a class of seventeen-year olds, I was presented with a number of very interesting questions. They were studying European history and so I was able to give my thoughts about the bravery of the many pilots who had flown in from all over the world to help fight the Germans. I shared my own experiences, how the War had presented me with my first exposure to American sport, after we visited a holiday camp in Middlesex and saw some US Army soldiers playing baseball.

I was a fairly well-educated and well-rounded young boy. Particularly considering the events of my childhood, I have to say that my parents (and teachers) did a great job. But, I was more of a "technical school" student than I was a grammar school one. I took the grammar school test when I was eleven and didn't pass. I took the technical test when I was twelve and did pass and went to Erith Technical School.

There were many things, events, occurrences, in my early life which I believe stood me in good stead for how I would be as a person later on. The times we lived through made us fully appreciative of the value of things we had and how easily they could be lost; and, subsequently, how hard one must work for the luxuries we had in life. We were working class, never anything grandiose.

Like many boys, soccer, or football, presented an opportunity—an escapism. From those days on the terraces with my father at West Ham United, to playing with my friends out on the street, and then, playing my first real organized games at the age of twelve, when I was called up for the school team at Welling Secondary Modern School. At fourteen, I was selected for the North Kent Schools, which led me then being selected to represent Kent. In my school side I played as an inside forward and scored a good number of goals.

Erith Technical School were members of the London School Association, and so I was eligible to play for the City team too. I played for London County Schoolboys against Glasgow Schools and I think I may well be the only person ever to have played in three of those games, because they normally happened only once annually. One year, we played two inter-city games, one at Hampden Park, in Glasgow, and one at West Ham United, London. For the second game, I was selected as captain of the team. It was a proud moment for me to lead out the team at West Ham United's ground; my boyhood favorite team.

At that point I got the opportunity to play for Dulwich Hamlet Under-16's, one of the biggest amateur clubs in the country. Whilst there I was called up to play for Surrey County, continuing my tour of the home counties. When I arrived at the district trials, my position was moved. The master in charge noted that I was the tallest boy and so he played me at center half. It is a trap that schoolteachers often fell into, and a theory that I don't subscribe to at all, but on this occasion it worked out for the best. Could I have made it as a professional as an inside forward? I'll never know.

When I was seventeen, I was invited to sign for both Charlton Athletic and Tottenham Hotspur Football Club. It was an opportunity I was not going to turn down, and even the choice between the clubs was made relatively straightforward for me as there was a London bus strike, on the day I was supposed to sign for Tottenham—so I was unable to make the journey! I signed as an amateur at Charlton who immediately sent me on loan to an amateur club in Kent, Maidstone United.

It was a steady yet admittedly steep rise but I didn't get carried away and that attitude must have helped as my local reputation begun to rise further still and whilst with Maidstone, I was selected for the England Youth team. I played in six international games against Scotland, Wales, and Northern Ireland, and then in a tournament in Nice, France, where we played against Belgium, Holland, and Switzerland.

These opportunities were as fantastic as you would expect for a boy of fifteen, sixteen and seventeen, but the truth was—as staggering as it may seem to some to read—that wanting to be a professional footballer was all well and good but it wasn't a profession that paid anywhere near the staggering amounts today, and that's even accounting for inflation and the comparison with other jobs.

After I finished at Erith Tech, Dad encouraged me to learn a trade, so I took an apprenticeship as a telecommunications engineer for two years, learning the occupation while on loan to Maidstone. I knew of a lot of young men who neglected their education and their studies to pursue their dream of playing football and if it didn't work out, they struggled. They had no formal education and so it was difficult for them to establish a career afterwards. I was determined the same wouldn't happen to me.

When I was of age to sign as a professional, I was also of age to enlist in National Service, so I signed as a part-time professional at Charlton Athletic and they arranged for me to be posted to Portsmouth so that I could still play. I played in the second team, mostly, but I was getting £6 a week, which was a strong healthy wage.

It was compulsory at that time to be called up for National Service. With my experience, I should have gone into the Royal Corps of Signals, but I was told by Charlton Athletic to apply for the Royal Army Ordnance Corps. When I went to enlist, they tried to get me to go in to the Royal Corp of Signals, but when they realized I was hoping to be a footballer, they relented. Apparently, it was something that was agreed with most professional soccer clubs and certain areas of the army. I had my interview and told Jimmy Seed, the manager at The Valley, that they were thinking of putting me in a different area, so he called their military contact and sorted it out for me.

I was in Portsmouth for eighteen months, allowed to come home every weekend and play for Charlton too.

When my time in the Army was finished, I had to make a decision, did I go back to telecommunications or did I take that gamble of being a professional footballer?

Jimmy Seed had told me in no uncertain terms that I would not make the first team as a part-time professional, because I simply wouldn't have the fitness and conditioning of a full-time player. I supposed there was an implied encouragement there, that if I took the plunge, I could be relatively assured of at least being giving a proper chance.

I felt I had earned it, though. I had certainly worked my way around the amateur and semiprofessional scene and once I was established into a proper position—center half, "because I was a tall boy"—then I think it is fair to say that my confidence grew too. From playing there often, I gather that someone along the way felt that I had good leadership qualities, or good organizational skills, because I was often named captain of whatever team I played in. I captained North Kent, Kent, London, Surrey Schools and the England Youth XI. I always found that interesting because I wasn't a shouter. I wasn't the most social of players, and maybe that was something identified by the coaches, that I could separate myself from that emotion and focus on the instruction.

I had good teachers who helped to keep me grounded and my father, too, was careful to make sure I didn't get big headed by the quick success I'd enjoyed at a young age. You could understand that I might—being captain of England Youth teams, my, what an honor!

I knew that my parents were proud of me and I think my sister was a little resentful, or annoyed at least, of the attention I got. My mum and dad would always go and see me wherever I played and so that attention focused solely on me was attention she was deprived of. I could understand that, and I also understand that she wasn't hateful towards me, she was simply frustrated with how things were. Perhaps my parents should have paid more attention to my sister . . . I'm not saying they were wrong, or did anything wrong, I just think that they neglected the opportunity to compensate for that lost attention, and at times, it showed. It was a lesson I carried with me through to later life and one I was frequently reminded of by my wife, June. Whenever our friends were blessed with a new arrival, we went to visit and if they had an elder child, I always made a point of first dedicating some attention to the elder one before going to the baby.

I think these mistakes, little errors of judgments shall we call them, are done inadvertently but it was always on my mind to ensure I remained thoughtful at all times.

Funny, then, given what I've just said—a little later on, after I married and was playing professionally, when my father would watch me play, he became very critical. My wife said, many years after that, that she felt he was wrong, that he had gone too far with his criticism. I wouldn't have said that I was a "mother's boy" as such but I'm not sure Mum ever took to June (or any previous girlfriends for that matter). She was a little possessive of me. I think if she'd had her way, I would have stayed at home and never married!

Included in the many life-defining events that happened to me while I was at Charlton was my wedding to June in March 1960. June was a Woman Police Officer. It was big news locally and our pictures were printed in the *London Evening Standard* newspaper.

June's father had left her mother when June was only three years old. Upon seeing the news of our wedding he contacted Charlton Athletic and asked to speak to me. He introduced himself and asked if I would mind asking June if she would meet with him. I did, and she wasn't too happy, but we agreed to see him and hear him out. He was very apologetic but I remember him very clearly saying, "Who am I to give you two advice about married life? But to have a good marriage you both have to give 51%." That advice stuck with me for the rest of my life.

Alan Brown, the former manager of Sunderland FC, had once given me advice on coaching. He said if I ever had a bad player, by which he meant a player misbehaving or causing trouble, then I should seek to get rid of him as soon as possible, because it was a bad apple that would cause rot to set in elsewhere. It was good advice and I applied it to my personal life too, as well as that piece of advice from June's estranged father. We vowed never to go to sleep on a problem or an argument, if there was an issue, to sort it out with urgency and always be prepared to give 51%. These two simple bits of advice remained with me. Good advice can be timeless when it applies to attitude and behavior.

I know that anger manifests itself in a number of different ways but it says a lot to me if someone's immediate reaction to a potentially inflammatory situation is to swear. The first thing it says is that they must have a poor vocabulary! But further, to have such a meek resistance to your own anger that you can only articulate yourself in that manner is a sign of someone who doesn't have control. I much preferred to observe and, to an extent, imitate, the behavior of those who behaved with grace. Walter Winterbottom, the England international team manager, and Football Association director of coaching, had this hushed way of speaking so that you had to be attentive to really listen and hear what was being said—and, when he spoke, you could say with a degree of certainty that what he was saying was worth listening to—and every now and then he'd raise his voice when it came to making a point that he really wanted to resonate. A possible teaching from his time at Loughborough University.

As I said earlier, it was one of the most enjoyable things I'd ever done, being able to make life a little easier for my own Dad once he retired.

I was able to talk openly to my sister about what we went through, though, saying it like that makes it appear like it was a great ordeal, we were both aware it really wasn't. I would say it was a standard, typical upbringing, and even though there was an element of the unusual with the attention my career got from my parents, I would still describe the various problems that came with that as those that are usual for any family where one sibling, for whatever reason at whatever time, gets a little more attention. My sister and I got on famously and we both got great satisfaction at providing our parents with comfort in later life. Tragically, though, she was taken from us too soon with ill health at the age of 52. In her periods of illness we became very close indeed and I suppose, then, there are some crumbs of comfort to be drawn.

two

Down in the Valley

I WOULD DESCRIBE myself as a good, honest professional. A good reader of the game, a good header (undoubtedly owing something to my height), and, as I've already said, a good leader.

I made by debut for Charlton Athletic in pretty much the biggest game I could play in, against Arsenal in a First Division game at home at The Valley. I always used to think it was 60,000 fans but it was actually 48,084; still, the highest attendance in the First Division that day. We tied 1-1, and I think I did a good job. I must have done something right because the press spoke well of me afterwards. That was at odds with how I felt. I was so nervous and anxious about (and throughout) the game that afterwards I was sick and literally threw up.

A number of factors contributed to how I felt. I felt added pressure with it being at home. Even seasoned professionals feel the pressure and tension of such a big occasion so it was surely to be expected. Furthermore, I was only informed I would be playing on the night Friday before the game. There were rumors in the press on Thursday evening. It's not always the case that you move into the first team in the position you play in in your reserve team but Derek Ufton, our usual center half, was injured, so I was promoted in my favored role. In practice games, Jimmy Seed had seen me hold my own amongst the first team players. I suppose to an outsider it would look like a bold choice to give a youngster his debut in such a game, particularly in defense in an era where center forwards were renowned for their physicality.

Thankfully in that first game I wasn't up against one of the rougher center forwards—that followed in my second game against Trevor Ford of Cardiff City. He was very clever, he'd always kick your standing leg when you kicked the ball. Consequently, you cleared the ball, but you finished in the dirt.

I took the experience of my debut and would later put it to good use later in my coaching career. Where possible (and sometimes with last-minute injuries, it isn't always) I would give a young player as much advance notice of their selection as I could. If all was according to plan, I would tell them on the Tuesday that they would be playing on the Saturday. They would then participate with the first team in training from the Wednesday; I'd show my hand with the team I was picking on the weekend, but I felt that was the right and proper thing and was conducive to the best preparation.

I know there is an alternative school of thought. Some coaches believe it's better to let a young player only find out at the last minute, with the idea that nervous tension will subsequently be at a minimum. Is telling the young player on Tuesday, therefore, giving him too much time to think about it? I didn't think so, and I still don't. It gives him a chance to prepare with all the routines, the set plays, and a proper opportunity to build relationships with his teammates. It's the best ammunition that you can give a player—information.

Playing in the top division of English football is a real honor for any player but particularly in the mid-1950s. It could be argued that the decade or so which followed my introduction to the Charlton Athletic first team was a golden age that has yet to be replicated or matched, culminating of course with England's World Cup triumph in 1966.

People enjoy procrastinating over soccer, with their would'ves and could'ves, and even in the ultimate triumph enjoyed by the "Three Lions" at Wembley that wonderful summer's day, there remains a question. Thankfully, not one of fulfilled ambition of Sir Alf Ramsey's side, who won the World Cup Finals tournament, but just how many of those who won it might have been long serving Manchester United Players if not for the Munich Air Disaster. In February 1958 when on returning from a game in Munich, Germany their plane crashed on takeoff killing 27 people.

In my stay with Charlton in the top division, one of my most vivid memories was playing against that Manchester United team almost exactly a year before they were tragically decimated. I was up against Tommy Taylor, the celebrated England center forward. He stood out on the eighteen-yard line at a corner and I went with him—as the corner was taken, he started running, and I followed shoulder to shoulder. It meant that trying to compete with him for a header was difficult as I was in an unnatural position of facing my own goal. He scores, and shortly after scores again, as United romped to a 5-1 victory with a Bobby Charlton hat-trick. During the game, once I'd realized what Taylor was doing, I decided I wasn't going to be lured into that false position anymore, and instead held back, deciding to give myself a proper run at the ball. My goalkeeper Willie Duff was going mad because I wasn't standing with Taylor and I was insisting that challenging him in that way was futile. Those goals had come very early on in the game but from that moment I was able to cope much better. I was learning on the job. It was a torrid lesson but a valuable one.

Taylor's clinical demonstration of punishing mistakes stood out for me as one of the huge differences between playing in the First and Second Divisions. You couldn't get away with anything in the top flight. Give just half a chance to a striker of that caliber and they would score without a shadow of a doubt. In the Second Division you could probably afford to give a full opportunity to a forward and it wouldn't be guaranteed that he would score.

The two best center forwards I ever played against were Tom Finney and John Charles. Tom was traditionally a wing forward but when I came up against him at Preston North End, he was playing through the middle. He had magnificent ball control and could change pace so quickly. John Charles, the Welsh international and Leeds United center forward was a tremendous player too, a gentle giant. He would go up for the ball and hang in the air. He didn't use his physical prowess nearly as much as you might expect. The former Cardiff City striker Trevor Ford may not instantly stand out as celebrated as the names I've just mentioned (although when he signed for Sunderland in 1950 for a fee of £30,000, it broke the British transfer record), but he was a nightmare to play against, using his stocky size to his advantage. He'd whack you for ninety minutes. It was a contrast to what I experienced competing with John Charles.

I was 25 at the time of the Munich disaster. As a team, we were devastated, because we knew these boys. To think we might play Manchester United again and many of them wouldn't be there sent a shiver down your spine. We were rooting for the survivors to pull through.

Here was a significant interest in how they would rebuild the club and restock their playing staff and we saw the footballing community really come together, offering players. United came back much quicker than anyone had a right to expect and although Sir Matt Busby got much of the credit (which he undoubtedly deserved) to my mind, Jimmy Murphy, his assistant coach, deserved just as much praise for his contribution.

There was plenty of talk about what the players who perished might have gone on to achieve and we had experienced first-hand how good they were, with that 5-1 defeat at home contributing to our relegation. They were so talented. Charlton and Taylor got the goals, but Duncan Edwards, a young 21-year-old midfielder, was imperious, commanding and, for one so young, dictated their game.

Of course, the disaster had a profound impact on even those who survived. Dennis Viollet was a tremendous striker and I had the fortune to work with him at the end of his playing career in my time at Baltimore Bays nine years after the crash. Understandably, he was very nervous whenever we flew. He never spoke about it.

Some never played again, including Johnny Berry and Jackie Blanchflower. Freddie Goodwin, who was a junior player, then became a part of the first team in the immediate aftermath. He worked in the States later on and I got to know him very well. The emotion remained, and again, understandably so.

I felt an enormous sense of pride being one of these select few people who represented a First Division club, and played in the first team. It really was a privilege and the opportunity to compete with players who were highly regarded international stars of the time—many of whom went on to achieve legendary status—was so enjoyable. Playing at some of the most renowned stadia in the world, too. Whenever we played at Anfield, Bill Shankly, their manager, would always be standing there when you came out of the visitor's dressing room ready to take to the pitch. I swear he received a signal when the visiting team left their dressing room. There is the famous "This Is Anfield" sign just before you descend the small narrow staircase, through the tunnel onto the pitch. Shankly would just stand and observe the sign, invoking a pressure onto you before you'd even kicked a ball.

I remember in the warm-up there once, a tremendous roar went up in the stands. I couldn't understand so I said to one of my teammates, "What's that all about?" He replied they'd simply won the coin toss to kick away from the Kop End of the ground, the Liverpool fans terrace, in the first half, so they'd be kicking towards it in the second half with all that support. The noise at winning the coin toss was as if they'd scored a goal. Even as an opponent it was a special atmosphere to be in. I never won at Liverpool as a player or a manager, the best I got was a draw (or a tie). We beat them 5-1 at the Valley, though, in 1957. We had a great record at home against them and a terrible one away to them at Anfield.

On the subject of great experiences, as Italy prepared to play Northern Ireland in a qualifier for the 1958 World Cup, Charlton and Luton Town were invited to Milan to play against the Italian national team in the magnificent San Siro Stadium. I marked Giampiero Boniperti, the Juventus striker. Italy was renowned for playing in a physical manner but they were actually hoping for that kind of approach from us, to better prepare them for their upcoming competitive game. It was a battle, as much as one can expect from a game that was still a friendly, but to play in such an arena against so many top Italian players was really the stuff of boyhood dreams.

I had some great experiences as a player. I rubbed shoulders and played with and against many great players but those early days, captaining the England national youth team, probably saw my peak performances. Maybe the reason for that is because from a fairly young age, I became more interested in coaching and how things could improve with the resources we had available including the greatest resource we have, ourselves.

Learning was, and believe it or not still is, very important to me. I enjoyed absorbing as much information as I could, although as a player, it was about developing my own game. I was fairly young when I realized the true value of taking all of this knowledge on board was so that I could hopefully impart it at a later date.

When I was studying for my coaching badges, I went through all the various procedures until I was appointed a Football Association Staff Coach and wound up at the National Football Coaching Center at Lilleshall instructing the coaching and managing sessions for other aspiring coaches—on a number of courses the coaches from Charlton Athletic were on the courses! I was one of the leaders here, the roles were completely reversed. So when I went back to Charlton, naturally, I was frustrated, because, coaching for the Football Association, I was seeing new methods of training and coaching that wasn't accepted at my club. I was always disciplined and never sought to rock the boat, if I did do anything, it would always be constructive.

In one particular session, we were doing a lot of running, too much in my opinion and I asked why we hadn't been given a ball.

"If you get too much of it in the week, you won't want it on Saturday," was the reply. I was astounded.

I could run like a hare—tall, slight, I may not be the quickest over five yards but I was a very good quarter-mile runner.

On this day, I set off and it was easy for me to break away from the group.

"Hey, where are you going, where are you going?" other players in the group called. So I'd slow down and rejoin the group. The outcome for me was that it really was of little physical value for me. On this day, I cracked. So I stopped, walked to our coach Jack in the middle of the pitch—he'd had us running around it—and said, "Jack, you could train a bloody chimp to do your job," and walked off. It was language that was pretty strong for me, and still is.

I showered and went home, expecting a call that afternoon, but it never came. The next morning, I anticipated being called into see the manager. Not a single word.

The methods didn't change. Sure enough, at the end of that season, we were relegated to the Second Division.

There was a tremendous frustration for me with our tactics and approach of playing. I was mixing with the best coaches at home and abroad. In the 1958 World Cup, Brazil won the tournament, playing four at the back. I suggested this formation to our coaches. It was never even considered. We played three, in a triangular arrangement. It presented a multitude of opportunities for the opposition if they could drag one player out of position, which they often could. The World Champions were playing four in their defense; we still hadn't caught on.

I was determined to try and implement changes and get with the modern game. In my very first course at Lilleshall I had to do a session and I didn't realize that Walter Winterbottom, the then England manager, was watching. Once I was aware of his being there, I got a little nervous, but I must have done something right or at least interesting because I noticed when he came over and introduced himself afterwards he paid particular notice to my name tag. As soon as I qualified, I was called up as the youngest of his staff coaches, alongside the likes of Ron Greenwood, Jimmy Hill and Jimmy Adamson, all top league managers/coaches. Sharing a staff room with these gentlemen was fascinating. Hearing their stories of their illustrious careers for club and country on the pitch and now sharing tales of our coaching experiences, well, to even be considered a peer to these men was a real boost. I learned so much from those times.

We were conducting examinations and Eric Houghton, a former great player for Aston Villa, was in the group I was leading. There was another player whose name I regretfully cannot recall, but I had felt he was worthy of a merit award. On the other hand, I didn't quite feel that Eric had done enough to pass. We were deciding who to pass and who hadn't done enough in discussion with Walter. With the first player, the other two coaches said that he shouldn't pass, and I bowed to the pressure of being outnumbered and agreed. When it came to Eric, they both thought he had done enough, but this time I stuck to my own guns and insisted I didn't believe he had.

"Walter," I said. "I don't agree. If you give a merit to Eric, then you have to give it to the other player, as he was far superior in my humble opinion."

Walter agreed to reexamine both of them himself later on. Alan Brown, the Sunderland manager at the time, was there and observed this. He commended me on my attitude and the way I politely expressed my dissatisfaction. Praise indeed for a young newcomer to the staff, and very much appreciated by me.

Sometimes perhaps more valuable to me that I was able to take on board was the value of preparation and the importance of conducting oneself properly. I consider myself fortunate, therefore, to have been exposed to those travels with the England youth team at such an early age. I wasn't aware of it at the time but observing how soccer teams prepared for games and trips in terms of travel, equipment itineraries, hotel arrangement, team discipline, handling passports, foreign currency and even baggage weight restrictions and policies when traveling overseas with a Football Association party was something that remained with me.

These instructions would be in a neat handbook which included a list of officials, coaches and Football Association staff on the trip, so everything was documented and nothing was left to chance. Meticulously outlined in detail for all in the party—team meetings, meal times, departure times, flight numbers—everybody was aware of exactly what, how and when. I was very impressed by the organization.

I was just as impressed by the provisions we were supplied with. Our training and playing equipment was all brand new and premium standard. You felt very good when dressing for games or even for training, and the Three Lions logos instilled this extra dimension of pride—even when opposition players and officials were given Football Association pennants and badges at banquets or dinners, there remained this real sense of pride of representing your country. Every aspect of a journey or game was covered in these itineraries; everything was first class in every way. It taught me the importance of a player to know that every aspect of game preparation was first class and well planned, and subsequently, the player would hopefully become proud to be part of that first class organization.

Years later, when I was appointed as the England National youth team coach, and when I traveled to European football coaching conferences, to the Football Association National Centre courses at Lilleshall, or when acting as a coach to FA representative teams these procedures were repeated.

Then, later, when I became a manager of professional clubs, I applied exactly the same kind of methods. The players knew exactly what was required of them at all times whether training, playing, or traveling. The club staff had that responsibility to organize and prepare all itineraries and especially good equipment; I insisted that we should get new uniforms two or three times in one season. I wanted the players to know that we cared and make them aware of the importance I placed on preparation, and how valuable I felt it was that they felt good and had a good attitude too. At the very least, I could always say that I did the right thing for my players, and that was very important to me.

I had signed full-time professional forms at the age of twenty for Charlton in 1952 and when I did so I joined a playing staff of fifty-two players. At the time, there was a salary "cap" which was fourteen pounds per week, and later raised to twenty, before Jimmy Hill, the Player's Union president, successfully campaigned for its abolition in 1961. So, players' wages were not an unnecessarily expensive item on the club's budget, giving the impression that players therefore were not very important. Compare that to the contrast at the FA and their organization and treatment of their players. I have to be fair and say that perhaps it had to be different. With only six international games spread over a season, that players had to be looked after when they went away, whereas at clubs, there was a game every week and sometimes even two or three.

Of course, it goes without saying that the changes in the game from the time I played to the modern game fifty or sixty years are too numerous to mention, so instead, I shall lay out exactly what we went through in terms of our preparation at club level. To consider that even then, club level was lagging behind the times, it gives you an indication of how things have changed. Selected team sheets were placed on the dressing room board the day before each game. There were very basic reports. We had to report to the home stadium two hours before kick-off time for a home game. For an away game, a time of the team bus departure for your opponent's stadium or to a main-line rail station for departure to travel by rail. It was basic and simple but no problem. Information about meals on the train or the ones we should eat at our home addresses would not be conveyed. The trainer or coach would inform you of the program for the team as the day went along.

We didn't see a weekly or daily training program. We just dressed for training. We went onto the pitch or went on a "Road Run" according to the coaches instructions. The first team squad and the reserve team squad would be training separately. It certainly was a message to essentially let you know where you stood. We did not have a training ground at the time, and it depended on the weather and the condition of the ground whether we were allowed to train at the stadium or not. If it was raining, it wasn't uncommon for us to use club's car park on an asphalt surface or told to run up and down the stadium standing terraces and around the stadium stands concourses. This was around the same time that it was commonplace for us to train without a ball.

Those interested in how big a role superstition plays in sports may find the following story intriguing. I look back and consider how simplistic and primitive it seems. If, as an example, we went on a "Road Run" through the local district and we won on the Saturday, it was one hundred percent certain that the following week, we would do the exact same run through the community!

We must have run quicker than usual one day. We had showered and dressed and went to a local restaurant for lunch. It appears that one of the club directors saw us at the restaurant and contacted the manager inquiring why we were eating so early and not training. From then on, if we were on one of these runs, we were told that we must not be back at the stadium until after noon! So, we now had the stupid situation that no matter how fast or how long we had run we would not get back to the stadium until after noon. If we were nearing the stadium too early, the coach (riding a bicycle) would just keep us running away from the stadium until the watch said noon. A First Division team training in such a manner!

I mentioned that maybe my own progress as a player was perhaps distracted or punctuated because of my desire to learn and improve and maybe that is the case; it could also be the case that these coaching methods, which I considered to be well behind the times, restricted me (and others for that matter) from reaching my full potential.

As I've said earlier, it really was no wonder that eventually we found ourselves at the bottom of the First Division and relegated to the Second Division. Football was competitive enough without putting in place these bizarre procedures that actually seemed restrictive.

So I learned what not to do just as early as I'd discovered the right way to do things. The contrast was astounding. The assistant manager in charge of the reserve team was a nice man but his language was appalling. It would be constant swearing, especially if the team had lost. He always had a post-game discussion, as soon as we were back in the dressing room. Too often they became heated with arguments amongst players. This after-the-game atmosphere left a permanent impression on me, for all of my career as a coach or manager.

It influenced my personality and approach. I learned from simple observation. As a manager or coach I didn't swear at any player meetings and my immediate after the game comments were always brief and to the point.

A "Well done" or "Good performance" or even "disappointing today" and often I asked the players to think about their performance and that we will all discuss the game at tomorrow's meeting. No immediate arguments with one wrong word upsetting everyone. No blame game, no finger pointing. Sometimes I would state, "Put that loss down to me" or "wrong selection" or "wrong tactics." I was not ashamed or afraid to accept culpability. I always felt that my honesty was correct and would bring about honesty from the players.

Another good lesson learned was the announcing of the selected team for a game. At Charlton Athletic, the team sheets were not placed on the dressing room notice board until training was completed on Friday morning. Sometimes, the team wasn't even announced until just before the game on a Saturday.

All players had to report to the stadium to discover if you were playing. It was ironic that most weeks, the team selection had been released to the press and appeared in the Thursday evening newspaper. My local news agent used to take great joy in telling me "I see that you are not playing this week!"

What a way to build a good club atmosphere and relationship between player and management! Yet another lesson learned.

As a manager, I would often announce a team for the weekend on a Tuesday. For in a practice game on a Wednesday, I wanted the selected team to have the opportunity to perfect tactics, free kicks etc., for the upcoming game. So many opportunities for me to learn what I thought was right or wrong and how to do things correctly and not incorrectly.

I don't wish to make this sound like a criticism of Charlton Athletic. My criticisms were of individual members of the staff, not the club. Furthermore, it was the people at the club at the time. The atmosphere and the camaraderie amongst the players was great. The fans were always loyal and supportive.

Today, you couldn't find a friendlier club. All former players are given first class treatment if you return; there are game and VIP lounge tickets for you and all your family. A welcome on the PA system is announced and sometimes an introduction onto the field of play before the game. You are welcomed and respected for being a player for Charlton Athletic FC. There are not too many football league clubs that treat their former players similarly today.

Jimmy Trotter succeeded Jimmy Seed as Charlton manager. In 1995 Jimmy Trotter had been the club trainer and I'm convinced that he only took the job because he did not want Benny Fenton, the other candidate for the role, to get it. He didn't want to work under a former player. I owe Jimmy Trotter a great deal of gratitude for it was he who gave me the time away to go and learn and explore the coaching of the game. Most clubs prohibit that through the season, but Jimmy was really good to me, giving me the platform on which I built my life. Enabling me to coach throughout the season, being able to coach Football Association teams in real competition had a tremendous value to me. I was able to cut my own managerial teeth and make mistakes in an environment where the spotlight wasn't shining on me. My time at Charlton was valuable in more ways than one, so though I am critical of the mismanagement and the impacts that may have had on my career, things happen for a reason, and consequently, what was damaging for my playing career was beneficial for my coaching career.

Nonetheless, relegation was painful. Jimmy Trotter flooded the team with youngsters—there was no experience in the half back line at all including me—in a league that was full of experience. The Busby Babes of Manchester United in the 1950/60s were an exception, generally, you would break in to the first team at around 22 or 23 years of age, and the game was a lot slower, so there were many players in their thirties. Invariably, youth will not get you out of trouble, and in football, you don't generally get into the first team unless the team is losing games or a player is out of form. If you introduce a young player into a struggling team, then even those players that have experience are so concentrated on the task at hand and making sure their own game is right that they don't have the required time to help out their new teammate.

When I was breaking in to the team, Benny Fenton was my captain. There was an occasion where the ball ran out for a throw in so I went to pick it up. In no uncertain terms, Benny shouted at me to put the ball down, so I did as he said and returned to my position in the middle of our defense.

In the dressing room afterwards he asked, "Hey, what are you selected to do, what's your position"

"Center half."

"Well, I play wing half. I'll take the throw ins. If you take it, and we lose possession, then we're both out of position and we're in trouble."

It was common sense but, I suppose, the kind of thing that is something that an experienced player does without thinking. The kind of mistake that too many inexperienced players might make in haste or anxiety.

Ironically, the following season, Jimmy Trotter tried to go the other way, seniors over youngsters, but it ended up costing us promotion. We should have gone straight back up into the First Division. I had played thirty-eight of our forty-two games, but for the last game of the season I was dropped. The week before, we'd walloped Ipswich 4-1, and the team had played really well. But, when the team sheet went on to the dressing room notice board on the Friday morning, my name was missing. I had been dropped from the team for the last game, and the biggest game, of the season. A win or a draw and we would be league champions and back in the First Division. Derek Ufton had been moved back as center half, replacing me, and Billy Kiernan retained the position of left half.

In those days, the twelfth man could only play if someone was injured before the game. I felt that I had earned my place, but didn't play. I didn't know whether to laugh or cry as we lost the game 4-3 to Blackburn Rovers. A few days following the loss and the disappointment of not gaining promotion, I requested a meeting with Jimmy Trotter and asked him why, after playing so consistently well during the season, I was left out of the team on that final day. He told me he had met with Derek and Billy, co-captains of the team, to discuss selection, and that collectively, they had decided that for such an important game, the need was for experience and consequently Derek and Billy would provide that. At 26, I suppose I wasn't classed as experienced!

Some very uncharacteristic mistakes occurred in that game. I'm not sure I would have made any difference if I had been on the pitch. A few years later, a former Charlton player, Jimmy Gauld, confessed to instigating and manipulating match fixing. I always wondered if our match that day had been one that he had been involved in and years later when I spoke to

Derek he confessed that he shared the same doubts. We'll never know—my most certain of doubts was that Jimmy Trotter had made the wrong call at a crucial time, but I could understand that due to his own inexperience as a league club manager.

In the late 50s and early 60s English football was on that rise that would culminate with the World Cup win. There were a lot of good, individual players but I felt that when it came to organization and formations, many clubs were behind the times. England as a country had been behind the times, they would often deride teams on the continent as being good in possession but toothless in attack. They couldn't score goals.

And then Hungary came along.

There was the shell-shocking 6-3 defeat at Wembley in 1953 and the comprehensive embarrassment in Hungary a year later when England lost 7-1. Soccer hadn't been around on the continent for too long but it didn't take them long to surpass us. I don't know whether it was snobbery or resistance but there's a brutal truth in there that the English game was being run by amateurs and major decisions were being made by nonsoccer people. Football Association committees consisted of school teachers, bankers and so on. That insular attitude came at the cost of harm to our teams and players. The resistance to playing in European competition is the perfect example. They weren't progressive enough. Worse still, a committee picked the team—at least, that was certainly the case when Walter Winterbottom was the manager. Imagine that!

three

Coach Jago

IT MAY WELL apply to many things in life but one of the things I believe to be most true about the game of football is that time is your enemy and your greatest friend. It is a commodity that few are willing to demonstrate the patience to give but it is proven that the greatest success stories invariably come after time was given. Arguably the greatest of them all in England, at Manchester United under Sir Alex Ferguson, came after the manager suffered some early bad results. But he was given time by the club Board of Directors. He turned the team around, won the Football Association Cup in 1990 and became the most successful football league manager ever winning 38 trophies before retiring in 2013.

Taking your time equates to better preparation and that applies throughout the sport, as far down the line as doing your homework on the owner of a football club that has just offered you a position or the player you're about to sign. I rejected advances from Tottenham Hotspur to become their manager in the wake of Bill Nicholson leaving White Hart Lane. If they could treat Bill like they had, after all he had done, then what would they do to me, a nobody by comparison? When I was a manager I would have a running joke with my scouts—I wanted their attention to a potential new player to be so detailed that I wanted to know what color pajamas the player wore.

I was kicked in the eye during a game against Middlesbrough when I went in with my head low and their winger, Arthur Kaye, had his foot raised. I had a black spot in my eye and it kept me from playing for three months afterwards. However, in the game itself, I was stitched up and sent straight back on—and, almost scored with a header!

Afterwards, I was violently sick and I was taken to Moorfield's Eye Hospital in London. The hospital doctors went ballistic at the club trainers—I had suffered a blood clot and could easily have been blinded after I was sent back on to the field. I couldn't train for a while and was not allowed to head the ball for three months.

During this time, though I was only 28, I decided that I should retire from playing. With my enthusiasm about coaching, I had been leaning that way anyway, and the injury made the decision easier. I played a few reserve games before the end of the season but my heart wasn't in it. Charlton retained my contract for another year afterwards but I had no interest in continuing to play. Even the fact that the money was greater than it had ever been thanks in part to the campaign led by Jimmy Hill, which I, as part of the Union, fully agreed with, it still wasn't enough to tempt me to continue playing.

Giving up for me wasn't as difficult as I know it can be for other players. I don't even know if differing levels of enthusiasm for playing against coaching had anything to do with it—but witnessing what I felt were fairly limited practices on the training pitch at Charlton (which manifested itself in a slide down the Second Division with promotion never a real possibility after that first year), I had a passion to change things. Being invited to attend European coaching conferences and having the opportunity to coach young national teams had shown me that I could influence, I could help make the change that I wanted to see. In many ways, that eye injury was a perfect time, and, strangely enough given the nature of it, it made me see things more clearly.

Jimmy Hill had just become manager at Coventry City and offered me the chance to be his assistant; I was also offered the Manager's position at Eastbourne United. Ron Greenwood, the West Ham United manager and my mentor, had been at Eastbourne, it had been there that he had taken his first steps into coaching, and if it was good enough for him, it was certainly good enough for me.

Eastbourne were an amateur club with five teams and working there also gave me the chance to continue coaching for the Football Association in a National youth team coach role with the Under 18's. It was a great learning school at Eastbourne and honestly, being a coach at national level gave me just as much pride and satisfaction as playing.

I feel I did a very good job at Eastbourne. I always wanted to play skillful soccer and it's not always east to insist on that when you start a new job, let alone your first managerial role. I liked to have players who were comfortable on the ball and like to pass well, ball retention was important to me. We had five teams from the first team to under 16s and I ensured that they all played the same basic way of good control, passing and movement so that when a player moved through the system or was selected for one of the other sides in the club, they knew what was expected of them. Fortunately, the players already at the club were technically capable, and I was able to bring in a couple more players from the London area who I knew would add something to the team.

We were successful, winning the Sussex Senior Challenge Cup almost every year, and we also participated in a league with the "A" teams from professional clubs. It was our aim to finish as the highest placed amateur club in the league. When the Athenian League expanded in 1963, it took in many more clubs, including us, and provided much more competition. We thrived. In 1967 we won the senior, reserve and youth cup championships that we competed in, the only time that had ever happened at the club.

It gave me great conviction in my methods, a belief that I could bring and establish success playing in the manner that I found enjoyable. It also provided great experience as an introduction to becoming a manager, the organization, that desire to have a structured culture and style running right through the club. Even in areas like spotting a player and how they might help your team, their individual qualities that you feel might help your current team or might flourish within it. I felt I had a good eye for selection of a player.

Of course, will is only part of the battle, it requires a perfect alignment of everything going right for you to have the exact balance in your team. It's a chemistry that every football coach strives for but is not always possible because the perfect player for you is probably also the perfect player for a dozen other teams and there's only one of them so you have to make the best of what you have. You're lucky if you get everything just right for just one period. You can enjoy moments or even periods of success without everything being perfect but those times where everything is as you want it are the times you most enjoy.

From my many years of management I think I would place the Queens Park Rangers team that I assembled into that category—the one I sadly had to leave (more on that later). Our system was so fluid and natural, with every player so comfortable on the ball, that whenever someone found themselves threatened in possession, there was always a teammate there to help out. It was almost telepathic. It was a wonderful rhythm.

Football with the emphasis on possession hasn't always been popular with the neutral supporter, or at least, it wasn't always popular until the modern Barcelona and Spain National team made it so, but it was always one of the most pleasing things for me to see. To watch it come together on a Saturday and see your team take everything from the training pitch into game was a reward regardless of whether it was in the Football League Division One or the Athenian League.

Maybe "possession football" has its reputation because it is sometimes perceived as negative and I can understand that but at least as far as I was concerned I would always instruct my team that their first pass was to play the ball forward if they could. If not, then pass it sideways. If there is no option there, then a pass backwards was in order. The way of the great Real Madrid team of the 1950s, and the incredible Hungarian team of the same decade were perfect examples.

Finally, England seemed to be catching up with the rest of the world and in 1966 they won the World Cup. The event was held in England and was a great occasion. I went to all the games at Wembley and found it a real delight to see the likes of Eusebio and Pelé, such great players, even though Pelé wasn't exactly given the warmest of welcomes on the pitch by his opponents!

As a self-confessed West Ham fan I took great joy from seeing Bobby Moore captain the England team and Martin Peters and Geoff Hurst score the goals in the final against Germany. I gained some satisfaction from having worked with all three in the England National teams early in their careers, too. It really gave a boost to British soccer as a whole.

There was so much pride in England's performances. Sir Alf Ramsey was great at picking players to play a particular role. It may sound peculiar, but I don't think that England played as well as I thought they could have in order to win the trophy. Sir Alf played without wingers, showing the virtue of playing to his strengths and having the conviction of his opinion. You never put players to a system; you put a system to the players. You have to observe the composition of the squad and make the most of the qualities of players. It's that kind of strength that led to the likes of Bobby Moore shining and yet saw the brilliant Jimmy Greaves sidelined.

For me, it was a tremendous insight into the character of Sir Alf that he was able to change from trying wingers to going without them in the middle of a major tournament where the spotlight would never shine brighter. It was a bold move and showed some sharp tactical acumen to observe the opposition and decide what would suit his available players.

We were playing a four-man defense, which, to me, showed that we have moved on and caught up with what other national teams were doing. Bert Tann, the former Bristol Rovers manager, had watched the 1958 World Cup in Sweden and upon seeing Brail play 4-4-2 had come back a huge advocate of that shape and so wanted his team to play that way. They lost their first three games in the new season and he scrapped the system, blaming it—that was something that confused me. To my mind, he hadn't properly taught his players how to play in this new formation, and he hadn't given it time to succeed. Of course, the question could be asked, did he know enough about how the system worked to impart the advice? Were his players capable to play that formation? It frustrated me because I felt that it was the right way forward. For me, Bert not giving the players the time to perfect the system was the reason that it didn't work, not his players.

Many wonder why England didn't move forward and enjoy another success on the international stage. That team was a combination of players at their peak and good management. But other countries improved much more too. I can't be sure that there was anything to blame on England's part. If we were guilty of anything it was standing still, while others moved forward.

That, to me, is a devastating mindset to have—one I can't abide. In sport as in life, I always like to learn, and I always feel there is more to learn.

It was fairly early into my new career that I became a father, when June had our daughter, Kim. Of course, becoming a parent changes your outlook on life. I had ambitions of success and those ambitions become intensified when you have a family to support. And for a while I would say that those changes, whilst ostensibly for the noble and positive cause, came at some cost. I spent so much time dedicated to the betterment of my career so that I could provide for my family, time on the training pitch, time spent scouting players to improve the team, that I never appreciated the one thing I was constantly giving away was the one thing my daughter needed most.

I must admit that I've never really been a "baby" man and I was a little guilty of not giving Kim, or my wife for that matter, the attention they deserved when my daughter was really young. I don't think that is a particular problem that I alone suffered; I think it is a common dilemma many men have when they have a family to provide for. Time, that most precious of commodities, gets lost.

I think I ought to go back a little and explain about how June and I met.

When I was at Charlton Athletic, we were playing at home to Middlesbrough, who had Brian Clough in their team. Walter Winterbottom was there to cast an eye over Brian with regards to his selection for the national team. I had an exceptionally good game. We were winning 6-0 and, perhaps naturally, we relaxed towards the end, and Brian was able to grab two late consolation goals. It didn't dampen my enthusiasm and so I convinced my friend John to go out to the Town Hall in Chelsea to celebrate. It was the time of the "big band" era and so every Saturday night was dance night.

When we were there I noticed a very attractive young lady wearing a "harem" dress and I asked her to dance. I had my club tie on, monogrammed with "CAFC." She asked me what team it was but I resisted as I didn't want to appear to be showing off—she asked me if it was Carshalton Athletic, and that made me indignant—that's like asking a Dallas Cowboys player if they play for Waco, Texas! I corrected her by informing her it was Charlton Athletic—I think she was surprised and (maybe) a little impressed. I asked her what she did for a living, and she asked me to guess—all the time we're having this petty back and forth, we're still dancing.

"Give me a clue," I ask.

"I wear a uniform."

"Flight attendant," I say confidently, knowing that many lived in the Chelsea area.

"No."

"Nurse?"

"No."

I was struggling.

"Cinema usher . . . bus conductress?"

She became as indignant as I had been.

"No, it's a blue uniform."

"You're *not* a police officer?"

"As a matter of fact, I am!"

As quick as that—though not due to the revelation, more, the change of song—the dance was over, and John and I chased two other ladies.

About four dances from the end of the night, I notice the police officer again. I was reasonably good on the quick step and the waltz but not so good on the foxtrot—the band would announce what song they would be playing next, and, it is some good fortune that it was a quick step, and so I asked the officer to dance. She said yes and as we danced, I told her that I'd been given tickets to go and see Tommy Cooper, the British comedian, at a stage show in London for that Monday night.

She sounded interested and so we agreed to go for a coffee after the dance with our friends. Afterwards, I took her to a large house in Notting Hill where all the female officers stayed—we used to call it the virgin's retreat—and agreed to meet on Monday. We did, and our relationship blossomed from there. The funny thing was, she had had two interviews with Pan-Am, and was awaiting the third when she met me, so she didn't go—she wasn't a flight attendant, but she could well have been! I often joked with her that she should have gone to Pan America and no doubt married some rich American gentleman.

One night early in to our relationship we had arranged to meet, when I received a phone call from her.

"I can't meet tonight . . . I can't say why, and I've got to go away," she said.

"Well, when will you be back?"

"I don't know, but I'll give you a call."

I honestly thought, and felt, I was getting the brush off. Four days later she called me and we arranged to meet. She explained she had been away on undercover police duty.

We were courting for eighteen months before we married. I still remember the headline, "A fair cop!"—she had short blonde hair. It was the start of a fifty-four year romance.

June was a good athlete herself. A terrific tennis player—she won the Metropolitan Police single and doubles championships. She represented Surrey at netball and had trials for the England Women's National team. She was such an intelligent woman, well-education and into the arts, and never too enamored with the game of football. She was proud of me for what I achieved but she wouldn't have minded what profession I had. Thankfully, though, she understood the demands of the game for me both as a player and a manager, even though I had that early struggle with knowing what was the right thing to do when Kim was first born.

A perfect example of that—Jimmy Hill had the opportunity to take a number of English soccer coaches over to Kuwait for big money on eighteen-month contracts. I was sorely tempted, but the only problem was that despite generous breaks where we were allowed to come home, it wasn't a place where I could have taken June, or indeed, any of us could have taken our wives. The security of the money, however, made it still a serious proposition, and I talked it over with her. Our daughter had just been born and having a substantial nest-egg was enticing.

"I don't mind being second to football, but I'll never be third to money," she said. "You can go, but if you do, don't expect to find Kim and me waiting when you get back."

Naturally, I said no to the opportunity. I didn't think she was being unreasonable. June put the family first, even if she understood the demands of football. When Kim was young, and I would come home from work, June refused to serve me my dinner until I had spent half an hour with my daughter discussing her day. No matter what. I could be starving, but June had her priorities right. And her doing that was crucial to the relationship I was able to have with my daughter.

June was tremendously supportive of me and the decisions I made within my career. As I mentioned earlier, she was also critical of my father's own criticism of me—she felt that he didn't know enough to be giving such feedback and I appreciated that support. She was so strong and independent and never shy in letting you know what she was about. She was like a mother and a sister in one to Kim.

When she was in the police force, she was posted at Notting Hill Gate; that was when she was looking to leave and become a flight attendant. Then, she met me, and she arranged a posting to Bexleyheath in Kent to live near me. She was bored stiff there as there was nothing to do, there was barely any crime!

Once we married, however, she gave up working, and put up with me for the rest of her days.

June was right about turning down the opportunity that Jimmy Hill had offered. People become infatuated or distracted by the material aspect of money. I'm not at all saying I was along that way but in concentrating so hard on establishing a career for what I felt were the right reasons, I neglected to realize the importance of simply giving your time, and, it must be said, June's intervention was crucial in that it made me re-assess why I was doing what I did. That enjoyment of profession which I have spoken so earnestly about was affected, when it might have very easily been compromised if I had concentrated simply on earning as much money as I could. Life isn't always black and white and even when you think you are doing the right thing for the right reasons, there are usually shades of grey which you must pay attention to.

I was not short of job offers and so even if I was to lament the loss of one opportunity, another would invariably arrive soon after. I was offered a coaching position at Plymouth Argle and two other professional clubs but I was truly enjoying the job I was doing at Eastbourne. So much so, that I gave serious consideration to resisting all offers to go into the professional game altogether. I planned to stay at Eastbourne and open up a shop. We had a beautiful house and a good way of life. I could run Eastbourne without any pressure.

June, again, put me right, this time encouraging me. "If" is a loaded word. You don't want to get to a certain point in your life saying it might have turned out better if this or for that had happened. And, *if*, you are responsible for those decisions, then you only have yourself to blame. When an opportunity came that was good for my career then I ought to take it. June was often right on such matters.

At Eastbourne, my ambition was to keep them successful, but also to do it appropriately. They were an amateur club. The dream was to win the Football Association Amateur Cup. It was okay playing against the likes of West Ham's and Tottenham Hotspur's "A" teams but Eastbourne were not suited to attempting to compete with professional clubs of that size. It is not disrespectful to state that everything has its place. Some things are good to go along as they are and that does not mean there is a lack of ambition. Eastbourne United served a wonderful purpose for me and many coaches before me and, as I have mentioned, I would have been quite content to spend much more time there.

It was flattering to continue to receive offers of work and when one came from Fulham FC I had to give serious consideration to it. Dave Sexton had just left as coach and I was asked to replace him, which was quite ironic considering what was to come later on. I knew Vic Buckingham, the Fulham manager, from when he was the assistant manager at Tottenham Hotspur and had wanted me to sign for them. Fulham were struggling in the English First Division but they had some very good players.

Vic had joined them a year earlier and cleaned house, getting rid of any problem players. There was not much talent or experience in the reserves or youth team and we knew that there was a real task on our hands. But there were some very good players there, Johnny Haynes, Bobby Robson, Allan Clarke and George Cohen. All international players. Those four were a huge help for me making my first steps into the game as a coach of a professional club. Any training exercise, then you could bet Haynes, Robson, Clarke and Cohen would be first up, meaning that any youngster had to follow by example.

Fulham was an ideal testing ground. I relished the battle, the challenge of having to turn something around. Towards the end of the season, in April 1967, we flew to America to play a friendly game. We played Manchester City on the Saturday and flew to San Francisco on the Sunday. We played a friendly in Oakland on the Wednesday against Honved, the Hungarian champions. The United States was having an introduction to European soccer, as West Ham was also out there to play Real Madrid in a friendly in Houston, Texas.

It was a trip that changed my life. Oh, I was impressed by America alright. How could I not be, with San Francisco as my introduction? The hospitality was wonderful.

We lost 2-0 against Honved and flew back on Thursday. Arrived on Friday, played at home to Blackpool on the Saturday!! Our long journey came back to haunt us and we were fortunate that Blackpool were struggling and short of confidence. We drew 2-2. We lost our following two games but just about avoided relegation to the second division.

We should never have gone to America. I can only think we were offered a lot of money. Still, for me, it was good that we went. I made connections with a few people and I think it was through this that Clive Toye, a former English newspaper journalist who was the General Manager of the Baltimore Bays, got in touch with me and offered me the role of head coach to the Baltimore Bays Soccer Club. I was getting £35 a week at Fulham and they offered me a $7,000 a year salary, which would more than triple my pay.

I had a long conversation with June because it would present such a huge change in our lives but she was supportive of it and so we made the move. That was the start of our American adventure.

four

Go West, Young Man

IT COULD BE said that even though the Baltimore Bays were in the North American Soccer League (NASL), I still hadn't made the full step up to what people would classify as a professional manager in the truest sense. I had been manager at Eastbourne United and first team coach at Fulham and the Baltimore opportunity was something I saw as a further opportunity to develop and do so out of the limelight of England, so to speak.

Players were going over to North America but it wasn't quite hitting the peaks that it would enjoy in the mid to late seventies. Soccer was still developing in the country. There were few professional soccer writers, nothing on television, barely any attention at all. The NASL had literally just been formed. The Bays had been one of the ten founding members of the National Professional Soccer League in 1967, and a merger was agreed with the United Soccer Association to create the NASL, which had 17 teams when it was first formed.

We settled in Baltimore fairly easily, living in a suburb in a nice part of town. Clive helped us to settle in our new home and we enjoyed a fairly comfortable first year.

We had a lot of young players and some Caribbean players who had speed to burn but lacked composure in finishing situations. There was a really cosmopolitan flavor, and I had the familiar face of Dennis Viollet to call upon as my main striker. Dennis was a player of tremendous culture and had been out there for a year already. He was so helpful with the benefit of that experience, taking on the duties of an assistant coach. He was class, quietly spoken, and had an impeccable manner. I oversaw a fairly promising first year. We finished fourth, narrowly missing out on the playoffs, which I suppose may have disappointed some as the Bays had finished first in the National Professional Soccer League the year before.

I learned so much from my time in America. Much of it, I hadn't expected to. It is often said that America knows how to put on a good show and their sporting events really can be spectacles but when you are given an opportunity to delve deeper into it and see what goes in to the organization of these events, then you develop a greater understanding and appreciation of it. That was certainly the case for me, it was a real eye opener and more than that, it had a profound difference on the way I would approach things forevermore afterwards.

I observed how the Baltimore Colts, of the National Football League (NFL), built their audience. The NFL was nowhere near as big in the late 1960s as it is today. I think the usual attendance for the Colts was around six thousand. What they would do is arrange to have buses pick up supporters from bars around the city and take them to the stadium. They would have their own names, "Colt Corral number one," "Colt Corral number two" and so on. And during the week, the Colts would have a player or one of the coaches go to each one of these bars and talk about the previous game. They were able to build their audience gradually through that sort of promotion, to the point where they had attendances of around sixty thousand. It was incredible.

The Baltimore Orioles were a tremendous baseball team at the time and they had these huge billboards around town which read "Get behind the team." All of the players had their backs and names and numbers showing in the image, and the only man whose face you could see was the coach. You'd drive a mile up the road and there'd be another advertisement on a billboard with the reverse image, the players all facing and the manager with his back turned. It was vivid imagery.

Of course, these sort of things were all new to me. But they would stand me in good stead a little later on.

However, soccer was a disaster. On reflection, it was the worst job I'd ever had. People talk about the crash of the NASL and they reference the 1980s but it was in trouble from the second it was thought up because they just didn't have the structure. In my second year, there were only five teams remaining in the league. We had to get foreign teams to come in and play an opening season schedule for us to provide enough games for the club supporters to attend.

The league office informed us that five professional clubs from England and Scotland would be available to represent each of the NASL teams in this first scheduled series of games, Aston Villa, Westham United, Wolverhampton Wanderers, Dundee United and Kilmarnock.

With Westham United being my schoolboy heroes, their manager Ron Greenwood, my mentor and with three of England's 1996 World Cup winners in their team (Bobby Moore, Geoff Hurst and Martin Peters) there was only one choice for the Baltimore Bays!

Aston Villa was selected by Atlanta Chiefs.

Wolverhampton Wanderers by Kansas City Spurs.

Dundee United by Dallas Tornados, and

Kilmarnock by the St. Louis Stars.

Even with these teams and many star players participating, attendances at the games were poor; at Baltimore, we average only 6,000 fans per game! And I am certain that's what influenced Jerold Hoffberger, the club owner, to make a huge decision.

There was a meeting in Texas before the NASL team league started in 1969 at which the Bays chairman, Jerold Hoffberger, said we'd fulfill our obligations for the year and then dissolve at the end. There was no conversation, it was his decision and that was that. We then flew to New York and when we got there Jerold said he was going away for two days but wanted to see me when he got back. We flew on to Baltimore from there, it was a long day. Frank Cashen, one of the top Orioles executives, said to me, "I have to go to a cocktail party later. I only hope someone asks me what kind of day I've had!"

I had the meeting with Jerold and he told me he wanted to close it down as quietly as possible. He didn't want any adverse publicity.

We didn't have any full-time players. We even had a few players that flew in from New York just to play the games. We moved out of the stadium and played our games at a local school in a pretty suspect area. The car park was torn up and supporters had to park in the streets. Invariably, the supporters would return to find their cars broken into and raided, or, in some cases, they wouldn't find their cars at all because they'd been stolen.

The club, or the franchise, was systematically falling apart, along with the league. I couldn't criticize the owner for his decision. We weren't drawing any money, weren't bringing in crowds, so what was Jerold to do? He owned the Baltimore Orioles baseball club and also was president of the National Brewing Company, and, as stated, did not want any criticism of his decision. Whenever he was in London afterwards, he would always call me and invite me to the hotel he was staying in for dinner. I think he appreciated what I did in the time I was there, and, hopefully, the way I conducted myself in the circumstances.

It had to remain a secret, I couldn't let on that the club was closing down, nor could I give any indication to the players or grumble about the obvious lack of investment. I took a lot of criticism from the fans.

Danny Blanchflower wrote an article in the *London Sunday Express* about what was happening and described one such event, that I was sitting on the player's bench and getting some abuse from the stands. "Go back to your Queen Elizabeth!" was one choice comment although they did tend to be rather more colorful.

It hardened me; it gave me a stiffer resolve. I consider myself to be an emotional and sensitive person so I may well take criticism to heart too often but I was able to at least realize that the abuse might have been personal but it wasn't for personal reasons, if that makes sense. I had the responsibility of being a coach but I knew the reasons for the frustration of the supporters were mostly associated with the very obvious and transparent demise of the club they followed, and, at the same time, I knew I wasn't responsible for anything connected with that demise.

Still, it was a very tough introduction to management, with the restrictions and so on and so forth. The lessons I learned were very valuable (though, I might add, nothing about the game itself) and gave me a very strong grounding before I went back to the UK and into professional soccer management there.

The NASL came perilously close to closing. They thought it would bring a financial bonanza after seeing the huge crowds of the 1966 World Cup but there was some terrible mismanagement and a lot of money was thrown away. Clive Toye wrote a book, "A Kick In The Grass" in which he slaughtered owners for their terrible management. I don't put Jerold in that category. I simply think that he thought there would be more of a financial return and he did not see the long-term benefit in continuing to invest.

It seemed that nobody in league learned their lesson, either. In 1970 the New York Cosmos were founded and were operating on a reported budget of $4M, which was an extraordinary amount of money then, but because they were backed by Warner Communication, they were able to justify the expenditure, and further, were able to benefit from the exposure afforded by the Warner Company. It was a level of promotion that blew even the hands-on work I'd learned at Baltimore, out of the water. They could, for example, send their team to play at movie premieres in cities around the world. It was attractive to the players and made the Cosmos the popular franchise that it was. The benefit to the NASL was that the increased attention brought more top names for supporters to see but it was done at a cost that was not manageable to other clubs and so the moving of clubs (franchises) or folding altogether inevitably followed. It was not sustainable. It finally went under in the mid-80s but came close enough to doing that in 1969 too.

The Americans had a lot to learn about the game but I had picked up so many ideas of promotion that I knew I could use in England, ideas that I knew would be perceived as forward-thinking because no one was doing them in the UK.

During that final season, I was offered the opportunity to join the national team staff. It was a strange set up. They didn't play international games aside from World Cup qualifiers and their federation base was an office on the bottom floor of the Empire State Building. Phil Woosnam, the former West Ham and Aston Villa player and Welsh international, was appointed head coach and called me to ask if I would be his assistant. I agreed, and we played two games against both Bermuda and Canada, winning them all. He had found players who were playing in St. Louis and the German American League in the North East and also a few from the NASL to comprise the team. Before our next game, against Haiti, Phil was appointed commissioner of the league, and so I was promoted to head coach. We lost 2-0 in Haiti and then 1-0 in San Diego in the return game. We were out of the World Cup qualifying round, and my role as head coach was over.

It wasn't international football as it would be recognized today. It was truly in its infancy. We had a squad of 23 and when we got to San Diego, we only had two goalkeeping uniforms in the kit even though we head three keepers. How could such a basic error be made? We had to send someone to locate a sportswear shop—fortunately, they stocked soccer uniforms, so we were able to get a goalkeeper's shirt. There just weren't enough good players available at that time. I tried to use my connections to find some US players that might be playing in other countries and discovered that Gerry Baker, the Coventry City forward, had been born in New York although everyone thought he was Scottish. He came and played but was unable to get us a breakthrough in front of goal.

Still, I was able to at least say I'd been a national team manager for two games. I had not had the best of experience but my confidence and conviction in the way I wanted my teams to play had not been shaken.

In the immediate aftermath of Baltimore closing, I had some concern about what we would do next. I planned to go back to England although I was offered a couple of opportunities in the US. I gave the matter some serious consideration before we discovered that June's mother had been diagnosed with cancer, and so, the decision was made for us. We still had our house in Kingston Surrey so we were able to return.

five

Arriving at Loftus Road

MANY OF THE major decisions in my football life have been made due to telephone calls. Of course in the sixties and seventies there were no computers, emails, and smart phones so communications were by telephone and letters.

In March 1970, having just returned to London from two years in the USA, I received a telephone call from Derek Healy, the chief scout for Queens Park Rangers (QPR).

Derek invited me to meet with the Club Chairman Jim Gregory and the manager Les Allen to discuss a position at their club. Being out of work and living in Kingston, Surrey, the decision was an easy one. Following that meeting I accepted the position as club coach.

With the 1969–1970 season almost over I saw the club's last regular season home game at QPR, a 2-1 loss to Leicester City. It ended a run of three losses and five draws from their last eight games which had dropped the club from second to ninth in the league. It was a run of form that suggested a change was needed, hence, the requirement for a new coach to be appointed.

The club had arranged a short two-week tour to Spain which gave me the opportunity to meet the players, assess their performances in the three games played, and gain a first impression into the chemistry of the squad.

It was very apparent that the squad was divided into two groups. The older senior players in one group and the young players in another, with very little camaraderie between the two. This division became even more evident when four senior players broke curfew before one of the games (an incident that would assist me greatly one year later).

In a discussion involving the manager Les Allen, the assistant coach, Jimmy Barret, the trainer Ron Woolnough and myself it was decided that there had to be disciplinary action taken against the four players, a fine at the least. With the chairman arriving to join us the following day, Les decided to discuss the situation with him and informed him of our decision before meeting with the players. Much to our surprise, Les informed us that we would all meet—including the Chairman—with the four players for him to inform them that they had broken the club rules. He told us that there would not be any fines at this time but if any further violations of club rules in the future would be treated harshly.

"A complete white wash," Jimmy Barrett stated quietly to me, "They're Jim Gregory's favorites. If it had been some of the junior players it would have been a different verdict."

For me, the new kid on the block, it was a good sign of how the chairman wished to be involved at times. Whether it was an *order or suggestion* to Les, we did not know, but it sent a message to those players as to who was in charge.

The 1970–71 season started poorly with only three wins in the first eleven league games. A short revival of three consecutive victories helped a little but the next nine games of four losses, no wins and five draws saw the team drop to 15th place in the league.

The atmosphere within the club was terrible and I certainly wasn't enjoying the situation. I accepted that I had to take some responsibility and I decided it would be best for me to depart the club. I had received an offer to return to the United States as head coach of the St. Louis Stars in the North American Soccer League.

With the third round FA Cup game at home against Swindon Town scheduled for January 2nd, I felt that we would enjoy a good victory and I could at least leave on a positive note. Unfortunately, another poor performance saw us suffer a 2-1 loss.

Out of the FA Cup, near to relegation, I decided that it was not productive for me to remain there. I was living a lie. I traveled to the club office on the Monday following the Cup loss to inform Les but was told that he was meeting with the chairman. I met with the club secretary, Ron Phillips, informing him of my decision to leave the club and asked if he would prepare my final salary payment and earnings details for my end-of-year tax report.

Just then, Les arrived and I informed him of my decision. He was surprised but then surprised me in turn by telling me that following a talk with Jim Gregory, he would be leaving the club, and that Jim wanted me to visit him at his office immediately.

"You know that I have released Les and I want you to take over for two weeks while I decide further action," Jim said.

I do not remember exactly how I felt on hearing that decision but I said yes and departed. St. Louis did not need my services until the NASL commenced in May so I informed them that afternoon that I would stay with Queens Park Rangers until Jim Gregory had resolved his problems on a new manager.

The following morning I met with all the players, told them of the chairman's instructions to me and that I would act as manager for the next two weeks. I informed them that I was going to enjoy the role no matter what happened and I suggested that they did the same. The past was to be forgotten we would deal with each game as it came and then in two weeks time we would all know of the chairman's decision for the future of the club.

In that two-week period we drew 0-0 away to Luton Town and defeated Oxford United 2-0 and Sunderland 2-0 both at home. Five points from a possible six, no goals conceded and most importantly a few smiles from the players, the board of directors and the club's supporters, plus, I confess, I had enjoyed myself. I felt that I had made some correct decisions on team selection and tactics and we had achieved some success. Following the Sunderland victory the chairman requested that I continued acting as team manager until the end of the season.

"I have a simple philosophy," I told reporter Jim Gaughan of *The Evening News* after the win over Sunderland. "No matter what your job, you cannot expect to stay indefinitely if you are not successful. In football everything depends on success. Naturally, any manager is disappointed when he loses his job. But you must know when you go into it that if you don't get results the club will look at you. They may bear with you for a period of time—but eventually, if things do not improve, a change will be made."

> "I enjoy football. I would not be in the game if I didn't. And if at any time I felt I was not doing my job, well I would not wait to be fired. I would walk out. On occasions disillusioned managers and coaches go out of the game and try to settle into other jobs. But they always attempt to come back because soccer is their life. Rangers have appointed me to run this club until the end of the season. It is my first managerial position in this country, and the club has given me the chance to show what I can do. If my running of the club turns out to be satisfactory it is likely that a long-term contract will then be discussed. I think this is the right course. If more clubs had taken it there may have been fewer casualties among managers. Rangers have given me absolute control and three months to prove myself. If anything goes wrong, it will be my responsibility. And that's fair enough."

"THE CHANCES of Gordon Jago, Queen's Park Rangers' caretaker manager, has of keeping his job must have improved considerably when his reshuffled team earned a point from their goalless draw at Luton," read one report from January 1971. Luton manager Alec Stock gave me a big compliment by saying that we looked like the best side they'd played all season. I had recalled Ian Morgon and Mike Ferguson, both wingers, in an attempt to add some penetration and, more importantly, some positivity.

Following the extra stability to manage the club until the end of the season that was afforded to me after the Sunderland game, I quipped to one reporter that I was prepared for the sack, though it was a comment made more about the nature of the game and the inevitability of transition—time stands for no man, after all—than it was about my sense of stability. Nothing could have been further from the truth in that respect.

An interesting situation unfolded, for with the St. Louis Stars awaiting my arrival in May, and my not knowing what might happen at Queens Park Rangers, they understood the situation and stated that they would be prepared to see what unfolded and they would keep the position open for me until the end of our season. I was in a very good position. If Queens Park Rangers appointed a new manager I had a job waiting for me in St. Louis. If Queens Park Rangers decided I was their man in a full-time role, St. Louis would accept my staying in England. For me it was a win-win situation, and I was aware of the good fortune I was enjoying.

After a slight lapse in performance—one win, two draws and four losses—the team enjoyed some new found confidence and with a run of seven wins, two draws, and only one loss in the last ten games we moved up the league table to finish in eleventh place, well clear of relegation.

It was a very satisfying finish for me and subsequently the opportunity to sign a three-year contract, my first managerial position in the English League, was presented by Jim. I will always be indebted to the St. Louis Stars for giving me a security of position at a pivotal time in my football career.

It was often said about me—and I said it once or twice, too—that I could easily earn a living away from football and that enabled me to put the pressures of the football world into a proper perspective. Another advantage to having that mentality was that it provided me with a freedom with my decisions. I could take what others might perceive as a risk, such as playing wingers in a struggling team, in my desire to see my team play good football.

My task when I was given the role as caretaker was to improve the team's performances and avoid relegation to Division Three. The appointment went from two weeks to two months to the end of the season. These extended periods of time were due entirely to the playing record of the team. On taking over the role as manager, my first plan of action was to put a number of senior players into the side in place of the younger ones.

From my experience at Charlton Athletic, I had felt that the inclusion of a high number of young inexperienced players (me included at the time) was a major reason for our relegation and I wanted to provide as much stability as possible. Of course it is possible for teams putting young players in to thrive but when looking at the best examples of Ajax and Manchester United in the mid-1990s, those young players were played in successful teams high up the table. It was still a gamble but not quite the same as putting them in a team which is struggling at the wrong end of the league table.

Having made my decision as far as that went, the next item was to select a system which would suit the players and also make it difficult for our opponents to score. We concentrated on counter attacking, and I felt it was important that we did place an important emphasis on that part of the game despite the fact that we were not in a great position, because that is the point of the game, after all. Goals. Zero-zero ties do not get you out of trouble.

With that strategy decided, what came next was instilling a belief in what we were doing, and the players seemed to respond with out great run of form that took us to safety.

Our plan had worked but to my mind it was only successful thanks to the scoring ability of Rodney Marsh. From the very first day of my appointment until the end of that season, Rodney was outstanding. He was our goalscorer and many of the goals that he did score during that period were due to his individual brilliance. I do not take away from the good play of the other members of the team, for without a doubt, our success was a team effort, but we all know that players with the same kind of capability that Rodney had were so often the difference between success and failure. The quarterbacks in American football, the home run hitters, the pitchers in baseball, these are the highly paid athletes in sport even today. At the end of the season, I received a three-year contract to be Queens Park Rangers' manager and I have always let it be known that Rodney Marsh got me that job.

Preparing for my first full season as manager, retaining the services of the quality players I had at my disposal was obviously of paramount importance. We started well, winning four, drawing twice and losing just two of our first eight games to put us in eighth place. It suggested a tranquility that wasn't quite there. In mid-May, I had received a telephone call from Joe Mercer, the manager of Manchester City, enquiring about the availability of Rodney Marsh. I dismissed the approach out of hand. There was no way I wanted to let him go.

City had shot themselves in the foot with regards the pursuit of Rodney. I anticipated we had a struggle to keep him—in fact, Rodney hardly made it a private matter. "The First Division is the only place to play football. The fact I am not there makes me feel very bitter. Rangers say they bought me as a cast-off. But let's face it, I'm not worth a good deal more than they paid for me," he was quoted as saying by journalist John Davies in June of 1972.

I had been public with my own thoughts on the matter. I was not interested in any player-swap offer. I did not want players that were deemed surplus to requirements by other clubs. "I have great respect for Rodney. I think he is a great player. But I do not want an unhappy player and if he remained unhappy I would do my utmost to find him another club. The board has put a price on him and they have said that if it is met then he can go," I told reporter Peter Barnard.

Later that month, I shared with John Davies the information about Manchester City's interest. "On June 6, Joe Mercer made an offer of £140,000. We agreed to drop our valuation of Marsh by about £20,000 if Manchester City would raise their offer by another £14,000. A few days later Joe contacted me to say that City perhaps could raise a little more money. I heard nothing further and on June 19 we called the deal off."

I was frustrated by City's approach because they hadn't submitted the formal bid Joe was suggesting was forthcoming. We were due to report back for training and I did not appreciate the attempts to unsettle my squad. Furthermore, I felt QPR had been more than accommodating in their negotiations. We deserved time to try and find a replacement for Rodney but City had taken so long that the players I had earmarked had already moved on. I was not prepared to settle for second best and I wasn't prepared to discuss the matter with Joe if they were quibbling over a matter of £14,000 if they were already prepared to pay ten times that amount.

Then, in late August, Rodney came to me and stated that he would like to be placed on the transfer list. His reasoning was that he wanted to play in the First Division and, further, that it was necessary for him to do so in order to get an opportunity to be selected to play for the England national team. We now believed that Malcolm Allison, who was at that time a coach at Manchester City, had contacted Marsh that he wanted him.

Naturally I was very unhappy and I refused to be bullied into selling our star player. I told Rodney that firstly, Alf Ramsey, the England manager, would select him if he was good enough, no matter which Division he played in and secondly, we were going to win promotion and he would go to the First Division with Queens Park Rangers. It wasn't enough to appease him. He persisted with is request so I told him that I would contact Alf and ask him if he would select Marsh for England. I did just that. Alf told me confidentially and only for Marsh that he had to be more of a team player, not just a very good individual forward. I told Alf that we used Marsh as a forward with no defensive duties but that he could defend if needed.

Hoping this would assist Marsh, I invited Alf to attend one of our games to watch him play.

Alf accepted the invitation. He came to a game and Rodney must have impressed him because Alf then selected him for the England squad to play Switzerland at Wembley in November. He was the first Queens Park Rangers' player to be selected for 60 years. He came on for the last 10 minutes in a 1-1 draw. Now in a position of some authority, I told Rodney that he now had his first international cap and together we would go to the First Division. This was at a time when the gap in quality between the divisions was not as great as it is today. I also hoped that as well as proving that he could play for England and be in the Second Division, I had proven to be as good as my word and that would be recognized.

During the following months Joe Mercer continued to call and offer figures around £150,000 for Marsh. I remained adamant, he was not for sale. It did not stop the dialogue and although I refused to negotiate, I spent more time speaking to Joe than I would have wished. I personally began to get the impression from our discussions Joe did not want Marsh; it was Allison who was pushing the deal. There was disharmony between the two and after some boardroom dispute; Mercer was replaced as manager by Allison. Mercer's bids, I remain convinced, were done to appease Allison. He was well aware of our Chairman's position; it hadn't changed or softened him. Jim had said "£200,000" hoping that it would deter City. The offers continued to come but still some way short, short enough to reassure me that Mercer wasn't too serious. Yet it had the desired effect on Rodney, who by this point had his head turned. It didn't matter that I had personally spoken to the England manager, that I had been honest and proven my point. Rodney simply wanted to go.

Manchester City was riding high at the top of the First Division with an excellent team. Marsh was our key forward and goal scorer and we were in second place in the league. No way did we want him to leave.

On February 12th we were in third place, just two points behind Millwall. The transfer deadline was on March 9th. We lost the next three games: first a 1-0 defeat at home to Blackpool, then a 1-0 loss at Portsmouth and finally, on March 4th, a 2-0 reverse at Bristol City. We dropped to sixth place in the League after that pointless and goalless run.

On Monday morning, March 6th, just three days before the transfer deadline, I received a phone call from Malcolm Allison.

"You are out of the promotion race, now sell me Rodney," he said.

I very seldom swear but this time I told him exactly what I thought of him in the best of swear words and put the phone back on its receiver.

It was clear, to me, what had happened. Marsh wanted to go to Manchester City and knew of their continued efforts to buy him. He had played in those last three games, but there was nothing in him, it was not the Rodney we had become accustomed to seeing at our home stadium Loftus Road. He knew that if we were in the promotion hunt we certainly would not sell him.

Following my telephone conversation with Allison, two hours later I received a call from Manchester that it was in the *Manchester Evening News* that Allison was FLYING to London, coming not by train, not by car, but by plane! His mission—to sign Rodney. I was furious.

I had barely got off the phone to the newspaper when a few moments later Allison called again to request a meeting with the Manchester City chairman and Jim Gregory for Tuesday morning in London. I called Jim and we agreed that there was not much we could now do. Marsh wanted to go and his performance had dropped so far in those last three games that he was almost a different player.

We met with the Manchester City chairman, another club director and Malcolm Allison at the Europa Hotel at 10:00 am the following morning. The meeting lasted 10 minutes. Five minutes for Jim to tell them the price was £200,000.

"That's a bit much."

"It's £200,000, and I have to leave in five minutes."

We went and waited in another room and Jim had made it clear he would leave.

After four minutes they knocked on our room door and the deal was then negotiated in about 10 more minutes. They agreed to terms with the payment to come in installments. It was an interesting meeting with them and then I was told to arrange a meeting with Marsh and Allison back at Loftus Road so they could agree terms, as if such a meeting was needed.

I knew there would be media waiting so I told Malcolm to come in around the back way on South Africa Road. I went through the front and was right—press were everywhere.

"No comment" was my response to their questions.

Rodney came to the ground and I informed him a deal was done and that we were awaiting Malcolm's arrival. When he arrived, that negotiation took five minutes.

I felt so letdown by these events. The transfer went through and we had a handsome reward for Rodney. Money in the bank as opposed to our star striker on the pitch. Undoubtedly, the money was worth it more than the player Rodney currently seemed to be. The damage was done.

We finished the season in fourth place. Only the top two were promoted at that time. If we had not lost all three games just before the transfer deadline we would have possibly succeeded in our aim to win promotion to the First Division. I am convinced that with a fully dedicated team we would have got better results in that short run. We finished just three points from the top position—two points, one win, from second place.

Our recovery in form following Marsh's departure was a testament to the team spirit within the squad, and I think to be brutally honest a few of them were relieved to see the end of the saga. Marsh, being the player he was, naturally got the praise when things were going well, but when things weren't, the press would say that we didn't play well because Rodney didn't have a good game. That was doing the rest of the players a disservice and once Rodney was out of the door they were able to regroup and show their quality. Sadly, the damage had already been done.

Since this was my first season as the manager, I really was disappointed and had great concern following the letdown. The natural worry was whether we could produce the same high standard of play the following year and would we be able to add the forward players that we needed to not only replace Marsh but to improve our goal-scoring abilities.

six

The Most Important Football Game of My Life

I DID NOT play, manage, or coach the most important football game in my life. I was seated in Wembley Stadium, London in April 1972 watching the German National team, led by Franz Beckenbauer, defeat England by three goals to one. It was a brilliant display of interpassing, movement off the ball, all ten outfield players with excellent technique in dealing with the ball and all confident in possession adding up to one of the finest displays of attacking football that I have ever seen.

That evening set the pattern of football/soccer that I as a manager and coach wanted in every team I controlled from that day forward. I knew that at Queen's Park Rangers we had the nucleus of a good team and we could commence to introduce that style of football that my assistant Coach Bobby Campbell and I had witnessed at Wembley that night. We noticed that Germany defenders were keeping procession of the ball deep in their own half and building their attacking play with a series of short man-to-man passes. We adopted the same methods in training, as I think most clubs probably did, but when it came to match day, they reverted to what was familiar, their old ways, long passes high into the middle of the pitch. It was our intention to take this possession style into games as well. This is where it is sometimes beneficial to extract and remove the emotion from the game. As an Englishman I was disappointed to see my country lose but as a professional I knew we could learn and, further, I was excited to see how I could put what I'd seen into practice.

With the 1971–72 season coming to an end and our club finishing fourth and just missing those coveted top two positions for promotion to the First Division, Bobby and I set up a preseason program that would take us to Norway for a three-game tour and then to the Island of Jersey for a final tour game against a selected Island team. We had one purpose in mind, "To play lesser teams." With no disrespect to the Norwegian and the Jersey teams we were of a much higher standard and our instruction to our players was to play possession football. The intention was to develop that style of interpassing from player to player and not worry at first if we played the ball forward, sidewards or backwards, just maintain possession.

Later, the emphasis would be to always look for the forward pass first, and if not there, then a second and third choice of sidewards and lastly, backwards. But from a coaching aspect, I insisted that my players be very careful of passing the ball across to a teammate because if it was intercepted, both players would be out of the game at that moment.

The key to our plan was to build a confidence in all our players to keep control of the ball even when put under pressure from an opponent. All of our training was on control-pass-move and this was to be taken from the training ground into our games in our first game in Norway.

We had a twenty-one pass sequence finishing with a goal-scoring shot by our center forward Micky Leach. The seed had been sown; the style accepted by our players and the confidence acquired to maintain the control, pass, move style. This much was confirmed by our fullback Dave Clements who stated in a press interview, "We did not revert to old ways of playing long passes high down the middle of the field."

Not that the results which followed were wonderful in the beginning, but slowly, I was seeing what I felt would bring success. Journalist Walter Bartleman approached me and asked me if I felt my players were tired after a sluggish 2-1 preseason friendly win at Brighton. Walter felt that the effects of our trip to Scandinavia were being felt on the energy levels of our team. "Not at all, although I can fully understand such thinking," I countered, "while there are signs of things we don't want and those we do want, we are coming to the new season with a plan which I am confident will bring splendid results."

And it did.

What followed was a fantastic year. Queens Park Rangers gained promotion to the First Division at the end of the 1972/73 season and our style of play won us many admirers. In our first year back in the top flight, we even won *The Sun* newspaper's award as the team playing the most attractive football in the First Division.

That can all be traced back to that game, England vs. Germany at Wembley, the most important game of my life. It was the beginning for a long and even though I say so myself, successful managerial and coaching career playing a style of football that brought joy to me and that always mattered most.

With money in the bank but instructions from the chairman that no purchases would be allowed until the close season, the search for new forwards began. Bobby Campbell, my excellent coach and partner and I started to discuss various potential players, and as luck would have it, we had a great good fortune at precisely the most appropriate moment. Brian Moore, the ITV Soccer commentator and a director of Gillingham FC, was a very good friend of mine, and he called to tell me that Don Givens, the Luton Town and Republic of Ireland forward, was for sale.

It appeared that Luton Town owed Manchester United monies on the early transfer fees for Givens and Jimmy Ryan and needed to sell to obtain the money owed. Gillingham FC could not afford Givens and Brian knew of our position regarding new players. I called Jim Gregory and told him of the situation and he suggested that I call Luton Town.

Harry Haslam, the Luton Town manager, was also a good friend and a quick call to him and an offer of £40,000 was enough to obtain Don Givens. I was delighted, for he had played very well against us during the season and was the skillful type of player that Bobby and I liked.

Feeling good, I called Jim Gregory to tell him that I had agreed the fee and we would meet with Givens on his return from a Republic of Ireland International Team tour of South America. It was on this occasion that I learned for the first time of Jim's fondness of interfering in player transfers. If he did not like a player that you felt could be of value to the club then he would refuse his permission or find an excuse not to sign the player.

When I informed Jim of my intention to sign Givens, his reply was that it was simply too much money and he would call Harry Haslam. Knowing

Harry as I did, I knew that he would not deal with Jim after already agreeing that deal with me, particularly when it was money that they needed quickly to settle their debt to Manchester United. Yet fortunately it must have been written in the stars that we would get Givens for Harry had departed on his vacation following our conversation and Gregory was put in touch with Luton's vice chairman to discuss the matter.

About an hour later Jim called me and stated that he had got Givens for £38,000.

I learned over the next three years that Jim liked to do a deal on all matters. "I have to see their eyes" was his favorite expression and if he could save a penny he was happy. It was almost like he had to have a challenge over money. The deal went through, Don Givens signed for us on his return from South America and proved to be a wonderful signing.

Our first replacement for Marsh was in place but we still had plenty to do if we wanted to be serious about pushing for promotion. I called Harry Haslam on his return from his vacation and apologized to him for what had happened. His words were "I know who was responsible. Tell Jim I will never do business with him again."

Thankfully, our second new signing was as simple as could be for the player Bobby and I wished to sign was a favorite of Jim's and he could not wait to do the deal.

We started the new season in fairly good form, winning one and drawing three of our first four games. It was clear that although things were going right, we were still adjusting to get things right offensively.

We had seen a player play against us for Carlisle United at the end of the previous season, and in fact following that game Jim Gregory had taken me aside in the Board Room and asked what I thought of that player, who was Stan Bowles. It was an easy answer for both Bobby and myself. I had purred watching him play, he was so skillful, could beat an opponent with ease and had a great left foot plus there was a certain impish manner about him. You could tell that he really enjoyed himself playing and there was an air of confidence about him. He was just the type of player both Bobby and I liked.

Following that fourth game (a 2-2 draw at home against Middlesbrough) I visited with Jim and suggested a possible bid for Bowles. Jim almost gave me the cheque right there and then, he was so excited and he instructed me to contact another good friend of mine, Bob Stokoe, the Carlisle United manager immediately. When I did, Bob informed me that Crystal Palace FC had just made an inquiry about Bowles and that their manager Bert Head was going to watch him play that forthcoming weekend. I asked what was the transfer fee that Carlisle wanted—£110,000 was the answer, £100,000 to the club and £10,000 to cover the mandatory £5,000 to the players union and £5,000 to the player. I informed him that I would contact our chairman and get right back to him. Jim Gregory agreed the fee immediately but no one was to know until we had met the player and agreed to the salary and bonuses and so on.

We were due to play Burnley away on Saturday so the club vice president Frank Vooght and I travelled to Manchester on Friday morning to meet with Bowles and then, if agreed, we would announce the signing that afternoon. Everything went without a hitch—Bowles agreed, Carlisle were informed and the press were notified.

I took Bowles to meet the team in Burnley and he made his debut against Nottingham Forest the following Saturday scoring a goal in our 3-0 victory, commencing a run of six wins and two draws n our following nine games.

seven

The Need a Number Ten in the Wormwood Scrubs Prison Team?

THE WORDS OF the title of this chapter were spoken by me to Stan Bowles, the outstanding Queens Park Rangers forward, at the Old Bailey Law Court not long after his arrival.

It was a poor joke. For one it would mean that Stan was going to prison and two, the £110,000 transfer fee paid for Stan from Carlisle United would be lost.

Stan and one of his good friends, Luton Town player Don Shanks, had been arrested by police officers of the London Metropolitan Police Force. It caught us completely by surprise and following phone calls from our club secretary Ron Phillips to the local police station we were informed that the two players had been charged with a number of counts including driving a van knowing it to have been stolen, driving a van without insurance, driving a van without a current driver's license, driving in a reckless manner. I lost count. There may well have been even more to add.

Both players had been released on bail. We immediately contacted Stan and had him report to the club office to meet with the club attorney, Ron Phillips, and myself to obtain his story of the arrest. Stan's story was that they had been stopped in the van by a police car as they were driving home from an evening at the White City dog track. They had been arrested, questioned and then charged but released on bail.

In answer to our attorney's questions, Stan stated that the van had been given to him by one of his friends from Carlisle to settle a gambling debt owed to Stan and he did not have any knowledge of it being stolen or uninsured. He also stated that Don was the driver and again he did not know that Don's driving license had expired. I believed Stan, and that these answers would be his defense.

It was not long after the incident that we were informed that the case would be held at the Famous London Old Bailey Court. In view of the importance of this to the QPR Football Club, Jim Gregory the club chairman decided to hire and experienced Queens Council Attorney to represent Stan. All meetings between Stan and the Queens Council were to be confidential and the Queens Council would only inform Jim Gregory of his views and the defense of Stan.

On the day of the hearing I was at the Old Bailey to be a character witness on behalf of Stan and while sitting with Ron Phillips the club secretary, outside the court I suddenly spotted Stan's good friend from Carlisle who had supposedly given Stan the van for the payment of a debt, sitting with two police officers, he was to be witness for the prosecution not in my mind a good sign for Stan.

A few moments later I was called into the court. The jury had not been called into court for we were informed that an extra count—driving a van knowing it to have been used in a robbery—had been added to the charge against Stan and Don Shanks and our Queens Council had requested a short recess.

Our Queens Council then informed us that he could not understand this action by the prosecution and that he felt that they had ruined their case. He then went back to his bench and with a law book in his hands addressed the judge stating a previous case which had set a precedent. He proceeded to bring doubt to the charges against the two players. Sitting just in front of me, the prosecuting attorney turned around to the police detective in charge of the case and appeared to speak harshly to him with regarding to the direction that the case was now heading.

At the completion of our Queens Council address the judge requested a rebuke from the prosecutor attorney and it was very evident that he now had a major problem.

Following his remarks the judge then addressed the court and stated that the jury would not be called into court; the case could not continue and the defendants were free.

The trial was over. Our Queens Council had won the day!

I will never know the technicalities of the law and never know the truth of that extra count that ended the trial but I do have strong feelings that it was not by accident.

Why such feelings?

Firstly, QPR had an asset, just purchased for £110,000, a huge sum at that time, possibly going to prison for a period of time and not available to play for the club. A big loss. Secondly, it was known that a member of our club had connections with the criminal world in London and also good police connections.

Why would the extra count be added to the indictment when it appeared that the initial indictment would suffice to prove the stated offense? Why the lateness of that extra count, being added at the court on the morning of the hearing? The reaction of the prosecuting attorney to the police detective on hearing of the added count?

We will no doubt never know how or why what happened on that day but we do know that Wormwood Scrubs prison team never got that new number 10 player. QPR did and enjoyed one of its most successful seasons.

With two new exciting forwards in our lineup and the team playing excellent soccer, everything seemed to be going well, until we suffered a devastating blow. Our 21-year-old midfielder Martyn Busby, one of our outstanding young players to come through the Youth squad, broke his leg in a horrendous incident in our game against Fulham at Craven Cottage. It fwas our 13th game of the season, definitely an unlucky game for Martyn. It ruled him out for the rest of the season.

We were a small first team squad in number and we did not have a top replacement. Jim Gregory summoned Bobby Campbell, chief scout Derek Healy and myself to his office on the Thursday morning to discuss what action we were considering. He felt that we should not lose the momentum that we had built and I must admit that it was reassuring to have the chairman keen to invest.

A number of names were being discussed, including Brian Horton from Hull City, with us thinking in the £40,000 range when Jim suddenly said "What about Dave Thomas at Burnley?"

At that time there had been much transfer talk in the press about Thomas going to Leeds and figures in excess of £200,000 were being mentioned. He was an Under 23 England international, interesting a number of clubs, but a concern regarding a calf muscle injury had supposedly turned Leeds away.

My immediate concern was not the injury, I was more stunned by the reaction of Jim, apparently undeterred by the hefty cost. Anyway it was easy to see Jim's desire to inquire of the player so he told me to call Jimmy Adamson the Burnley manager right there and then. Jimmy told me that the player was available for transfer. Burnley had a reputation of developing young players then selling them in order to finance the club. I asked Jimmy Adamson if we could let our chairman contact their chairman to negotiate any deal for they were the men who were going to decide the price and any terms. He agreed. It was fascinating to hear these two men negotiate over the phone, Jim Gregory and Bob Lord, the Burnley chairman, and much to my surprise they agreed to a fee of £162,000. In his mind, Jim thought he was getting a bargain, and he loved that.

This was Thursday and if we wanted to play him on Saturday against Sunderland we had to have him registered with the FA and the Football League by 3pm on Friday.

We got Dave Thomas to London late Thursday night. I had been at a local black tie social dinner dance and had to leave it in order to meet Dave at my home. We agreed on terms, had a medical on Friday morning and had the papers registered so that he could play at Loftus Road against Sunderland on the Saturday afternoon. Late on that Thursday, Dave's face had been a picture when he saw me dressed up to the nines. I told him that's what we did for every new signing for over £100,000! We sat in the kitchen negotiating the terms and it took no longer than twenty minutes. I think our position in the league helped persuade him.

I called Jim to tell him the good news.

"Any extra?" he asked.

That's what he normally asked when we signed a player. I don't know what he'd been used to before, although I know exactly what he meant, he wanted to know if I'd had to pay a sweetener on top of the salary and bonuses. I wasn't into that and repeated that to Jim. He was as happy as could be.

I recounted my anecdote about wearing the black tie and what I'd said to Dave, and Jim said, "You should have told him that you have to wait tables and that's how we've been able to afford him!" It was an anecdote shared in one of the late Brian Woolnough's columns. Inside that column was a quote from me "If Rangers don't improve after every season then I will have failed."

And that was how I felt. Those weren't bullish words. I felt that was the purpose of the job!

We ended up paying £162,000 for Dave Thomas, on top of the £110,000 for Bowles and £38,000 for Don Givens. Over three hundred thousand pounds. I did not sleep for a week!

The three signings completed our team but credit must also go to the likes of Gerry Francis and Terry Venables, who was enjoying the best season of his career to date, and at the end of a brilliant season, promotion to the First Division was achieved.

We had done it playing the right way. One newspaper report from October, when we had played at Aston Villa, read

> "Queen's Park Rangers trampled Villa to their first home defeat of the season on Saturday. But it was the style of their football as much as their obvious talent which stunned Villa Park into near silence. Here was a side, playing away from home in a vital Second Division promotion battle, and coming out to attack. And that, say Rangers, is the answer to defensive football. They argue that clubs are so used to visiting sides spreading a line of defenders across the field that they are taken by surprise when they are put under pressure themselves. And Rangers are doing it with an attractive blend of possession and swift breaks for goal."

To win such praise for a game we only won 1-0 spoke volumes about the way we were playing.

We had gained promotion with four games still to go and although we won all four of those last games, we still did not catch Burnley for the top spot and the Championship but we were in the First Division. Our promotion was guaranteed with a goalless draw at Cardiff. It was uncharacteristic of us not to score but it was most certainly the best goalless draw of my career! To get over the line and into the top flight was a wonderful feeling. I recall my immense satisfaction t being one of a select few to play in the top flight and I was now one of the 22 managers of the English First Division—a very proud moment in my soccer career.

eight

Mixing with the Big Boys

SATISFACTION AT BEING promoted did not translate into any complacency. In August 2014, David Owen of the *Financial Times* wrote for "Inside World Football" of one of his stories way back in 1974 that the UK's loss was the USA's gain with regards to the fact that I spent much of my managerial career in North America.

I share these words with you not to crow, or boast, but because David's article shared words I had said but had forgotten.

"We don't just want Dad and the older kids to come along," I am quoted as saying in 1974.

> "We want Mum, too, with first-class facilities for leaving the toddlers in expert care while she watches. Above all—with such possible innovations as bars, tea and coffee lounges, restaurants, and clubs-within-the-club—we want the place used every day—not just match days. We want to sell Rangers to folk not just as their friendly local football club but also as their friendly local meeting place. We want them to get, and feel, involved with us."

I share those words because although they were uttered in 1974, I am minded to return to the first few weeks following my agreement to take over permanently at Loftus Road, and a press conference I held to announce a "Meet The Players" day.

> "This is something we feel we want to do; something extra to thank season ticket holders. We want to give them the chance to meet the players and know them a little better, and also give them a chance to see what we do behind the scenes. This is not a gimmick. We really want to thank these supporters who pay their money at the beginning of the season . . . let's face it, they don't know what kind of football they are going to see. We want them to know we appreciate this."

That same summer I attended a forum with QPR Supporter's Club secretary Daphne Biggs, treasurer Ken Blackburn and committee member John Kennedy to answer questions. To demonstrate my transparency, journalist Alan Williams was also invited and printed the transcript of the interview in his newspaper.

On the subject of assisting with cheaper travel to away matches:

> "I have been having talks with a travel company on this subject. I understand we need in the region of 200 supporters to make it much cheaper. I realize we can't do this until we get more people to travel. Maybe we have got to win a few more matches before this happens."

On improvements in the ground such as tea bars:

> "I have attempted to improve the facilities within a budget. After all I have got to balance the books. Many clubs are paying out more nowadays than they are bringing in. But we must bring the fans in and cater for them . . . I know that toilet facilities of many clubs in the League are appalling and I would like to improve them here. But I have my problems and this can't be done overnight."

On women supporters playing a part in the future of the club:

> "Every supporter is important to me and remember, every woman supporter can bring a man to a match. But I realize we can only attract the women if we improve the facilities."

In the summer of 1973, Michael Hart of the *Evening Standard* newspaper was another to report on my very public intention of bringing US-style promotions to the British shores.

"At Baltimore they embarked on a massive campaign, involving staff and public," I was quoted as saying.

> "First, they insisted that every footballer on the staff lived in the city. Then they sent out each player to meet the public. They sent them to lunches, the Rotarians, the social clubs, dinner parties, receptions, everything. The idea was to get the players involved with the people, to build up a relationship between the club and the public. It worked beautifully. The public eventually weren't going to see a footballer with a number on his back. They were going to see Joe or Bill, their friend from around the corner. They knew the men out on the field. The gridiron clubs in America also have films which the player shows to fans (at meetings). We're preparing the same sort of thing. We're going to have QPR films and have players talk through them. Another American idea we're employing is the sale of season tickets to big businesses and commerce."

So it wasn't necessarily promotion that enabled me to initiate the implementation of practices I had witnessed in Baltimore but with a certain amount of time at QPR, and now understanding the club and its fan base more intricately, I had observed where and how the club could benefit. Make no mistake, the primary goal for these ideas was to increase the supporter base of the club which would in turn boost the coffers, so to speak, but what I had recognized in America was a greater relationship developed between the supporters and their club with the corresponding closeness they felt.

It's for others to speculate how applying all of the ideas such as restaurants and coffee shops might have helped with regards to the hooligan culture which was prevalent at the time and perhaps there was some resistance to the ideas from both sides because of that, but what I am able to say for certain is that what we did worked at QPR. We had tremendous success.

David Own also generously credited me with successfully overseeing a period of transition following the sale of Rodney Marsh, likening it to the difficulties faced by Tottenham after losing Gareth Bale, and Liverpool after selling Luis Suarez. Our transition was similarly seismic and fortunately ultimately successful but our ambition was greater after promotion in 1973. Our fee for selling Rodney was just £200,000, measly by comparison. Some players today receive that as a weekly wage!

Further to that, at least Tottenham and Liverpool were able to immediately reinvest. I remember quite clearly being told by Jim Gregory,

> "You do not have any monies to spend on new players until the end of the season or the start of next season. Do your homework on possible new signings and select players who will not only gain us promotion to the First Division but will keep us there. If we move to sign new players now, the prices will be high, for everyone knows that we have money in the bank."

It was sound advice as history proved he was right but he did not speak with the benefit of hindsight nor an aggregation of examples to justify his reasoning. Perhaps Jim Gregory's advice ought to have been given to Brendan Rodgers to spend £25m on Adam Lallana and £20m on Dejan Lovren, both of Southampton, in the wake of selling Suarez.

Perhaps the best example is still at Liverpool but going back to when they sold Fernando Torres to Chelsea for £50m. It was intensified by the fact that the "transfer deadline day" created a temporary false economy but they still willingly paid £37m for Newcastle United forward Andy Carroll. Whether or not you think the players were overpriced is a matter of personal opinion but surely it stands to reason that the reason for many of these fees is simply because the selling club is aware of how much money the buying club has?

We sat tight and bided our time after selling Rodney. Though when the time came, and we bought Given, Bowles and Thomas for a combined expenditure of £312,000, like I said, it gave me a few sleepless nights. Still, if we had moved in the immediate aftermath of selling Marsh to Manchester

City, I'm convinced that each of those players would have cost us a far more princely sum.

I would have had a problem had I even tried. Remember, Rodney was sold on the Monday before a Thursday transfer deadline. Although I was aware of what was happening, the speed of proceedings and the timing of them coming so late in the season as they did, caught me by surprise and with no adequate time to find a replacement anyway.

Before I was named permanent manager, I had taken the players aside in training to tell them that they should work for Rodney. This came after some outside criticism that he didn't defend as much as he should. Up front, he had a gift, that knack of scoring goals, and as long as he continued to do that, I said, we should pull together and do the defensive work for him. However, I warned that if Rodney's form dipped and the goals dried up, he better start doing some defensive duties.

"But I'm not a player. You're the players. Do you accept this?"

Of course, the players were professional about it and were not going to say "no," but I think some of them, particularly the younger ones like Gerry Francis, resented the situation. Francis was proving a very capable player in his own right and didn't seem to appreciate it always being about Rodney, win, lose or draw. Life after Marsh was good for Gerry as it was for the squad who were able to prove themselves with promotion. Gerry was the most rapidly improved young player I'd ever seen, from breaking into the side at 17 to when he was 21. His development was phenomenal and certainly helped by the departure of Marsh.

Still, I'd always thought that we couldn't replace what Marsh brought to the team with just one player. It turned out that we probably could have with Bowles, but with Givens and Thomas, we had a number of quality players at our disposal. Thomas had tons of lethal speed and Bowles could go past players as if they weren't there. It was a combination, backed up by Francis and Leach, which provided a goalscoring machine. We had eleven players who could play the football I wanted them to. To have Clement, Gillard, Francis, Bowles, Phil Parkes and Terry Mancini all gaining international recognition during this period; what an achievement.

Our form had been so exceptional. We weren't just winning games, but we were playing so well and full of confidence.

Terry Venables had been a fine player for us and a great captain, a great leader. I should have kept him and made him coach. He might not have wanted that, he obviously had his own ambitions of being a manager. At that time he had an ankle injury and when Malcolm Allison who was now manager of Crystal Palace, approached us to purchase him, Terry came to me, aware of the approach and said that he didn't expect to play on beyond the summer because of the injury and he wanted to go. I allowed it. I remain good friends with Terry but I must ensure that the record is straight with that because he later wrote a book and said he didn't know why I sold him. He was the one who came to me! I thought I was doing the right thing for him.

By that time, of course, I'd signed McLintock from Arsenal, and he had captained them in 1970 to a First Division championship and FA Cup "Double" so was certainly capable of being the leader we needed. We had Terry Mancini who was a good player but unlike Frank McLintock, could not move forward on the attack with the ball. We would instruct Terry to give the ball to Venables or Francis as quickly as possible. His strength was battling in the air or winning tackles.

I first heard that for whatever reason, Arsenal weren't going to give Frank McLintock a testimonial, but instead, would make him available for transfer for a very low fee of £25,000. Naturally there was a lot of interest in him. I contacted Frank and told him to go and see all of the interested clubs and leave us until last. He did that and when he came to me, I told him what he'd just done had essentially been a waste of time, because he was going to sign for us.

"I'll tell you why," I continued, although I confess Frank must have thought I was quite big-headed. "We're on the way up, we're getting promoted, and you are ideal for us as a leader and for the style of football we want to play. And lastly, how many children have you got?"

"Five," he replied.

"They can still live in the same house, same area, go to the same school. You go to West Bromich Albion, or any of the other clubs interested, what are you going to do?"

I had persuaded him to discuss terms and so he went to see Jim Gregory, who spoke the language of cash and was able to convince Frank to sign. I had my Beckenbauer. I have to give Jim credit for getting that deal done, just as he did with Dave Thomas. As manager I was just happy to have very good players in my squad.

Despite having nothing to play for in the last four games in Division Two, we won them all, giving us a tremendous momentum and confidence going into the following year. A consequence of everything coming together was that the players now had a greater belief in the methodology of Bobby Campbell and myself. We had wanted to play a certain style and they now fully believed in their capability to do it. Because we placed so much emphasis on technical ability, the self-confidence of the players grew.

Call it confidence, call it bullishness, but with McLintock completing the team, I was sure we didn't need any more new players. Our team, our boys, were good enough to contend with the First Division heavyweights, and not even the change in regulations that increased the number of relegated teams to three dampened our spirits.

The first team picked itself and were reliable ... now, confidence is a fragile yet tremendously important aspect of sport, but by trusting the same group of players to play at a high level and telling them that I expected them to not only keep us in the division but play as well as they had in Division Two, I think that helped them even more when it came to starting our new adventure. We couldn't give false praise. I couldn't tell Mancini he could be McLintock, for example. But I think it all worked so well because the balance was perfect.

In Dave Thomas we had a penetrative force which we knew could reap dividends. He was the kind of player that the man on the terrace wanted to see, he could take the ball to our opponents penalty area, find space to wrap his left foot around the ball and cross it into the goal area. I wanted him to maintain the confidence to attack our opponents in this new league.

"It doesn't matter if you only get past them three or four times out of ten," I reassured him, "in those three or four times you'll cause enough damage to win us the game."

Just as importantly as instilling that confidence and belief was that unwavering insistence that I wanted my team to play football in the right way. I did consider bringing in a higher caliber of player but if I was going to do it, I wanted it to be a statement, in much the same way that McLintock had been. So for a while I was interested in George Best, one of footballs greatest ever entertainers, whose time at Manchester United was coming to an end. Ultimately we decided against it, but even in doing that, we were showing how far we had come. How many clubs, when presented with the real possibility of signing one of the game's greatest players, can be bold enough to say no? Given George's off the field problems of discipline and accusations of a very active night life at the time there was no denying it would be a risk to have taken him. It was still a risk to pass up on the opportunity. It had also been discussed that George's presence could have attracted up to 10,000 extra supporters. We were keen to boost attendances and capitalize on the kind of interest that saw us attract 2,500 supporters to our first training session of the season.

Yet despite those upsides to bringing in George, I was concerned that the potential negative impact would disrupt all the good things that we had built, although, I have to be honest and say we didn't adapt swimmingly to life in the First Division. We did find it tough and took a while to find our feet but I was satisfied and encouraged that the players were brave enough to remain faithful to the style of football which we had become accustomed to. We drew four and lost one of our first five league games, after losing against Luton Town and Millwall in preseason exhibition games.

But the signs were there. Our only loss in those five league games had been at Old Trafford, hardly a cause for huge concern as far as I was concerned, even if supporters were now beginning to fear a replication of the clubs previous season in Division One where Queens Park Rangers had set a record lowest points total in relegation.

Slowly but surely we got over the shock of that step up, and that nervous tension which I think naturally exists when a team gets promoted, began to ease. We won 3-2 at West Ham with Givens scoring twice to record our first win of the season. We scored three in another win at Newcastle. And when we defeated Arsenal 2-0, giving the club its first win over the Gunners in more than fifty years, it gave the players a renewed belief that they were not only doing well, they were making history.

We may have won the points but we lost Bobby Campbell to Arsenal. He had been frustrated that we didn't receive a correct increase in salaries for gaining promotion and of course, Arsenal were such a big club. But

Frank Sibley my reserve team coach assumed more responsibility and I was heartened and reassured by the wonderful seniority displayed by Venables and McLintock. McLintock told the reporter James Lawton, "There's no point in glossing over the fact that I was sorry to see Campbell go. He's a good man. But there is something in this club which goes beyond coaching efficiency. It's the attitude of these players right through the week."

Frank was doing himself a disservice by not including himself in that. Their attitude towards improvement was shining through in matches. We scored eight goals in a League Cup game against Sheffield Wednesday. We had been working on a free kick routine with Givens where he would receive the ball on the ground and play it off low to Leach. We had tried it a few times and it wasn't working. The players decided to try something different, and so Givens would play it in the air as opposed to low. Terry Venables was the taker of the free kick and it was vital to the move that it was delivered firmly and with pace. In this game, it worked wonderfully, and Leach met Givens' pass with a fantastic volley. Perfect. They all came running towards the bench to celebrate with the coaches—what a communal triumph. Yet the innovation, the change, had come from the players, not the coaches. They deserved all the credit. It was a goal that summed up our collective efforts and I'm not sure our fans understood why we celebrated that goal, out of the eight on the night, with such particular exuberance.

It inspired a desire for improvement in other players. I remember seeing Clement and Gillard staying behind after training to work with the "walls on wheels" and practice free kicks in the same way. It was a joy to be working among players with such an attitude.

Going into Christmas, we found ourselves in sixth place after another win, 3-2, over Newcastle. We welcomed Manchester United on New Year's Day and beat them comfortably 3-0. They were having a lot of problems but it was a great victory and a famous day which showed how far we had come. Tommy Docherty described us "far and away the best team" they had played that season. A nice compliment.

It was not long after we had considered that move for Best. I was confident that we could provide him with an environment that would help him rediscover his love for the game and that talent we all knew he had, and there is no doubt that it would have been a huge signing for the club. Jim would have been salivating at the thought of bringing him in. But George went on one of his disappearing acts, leaving United in the middle of the season, and that was enough to put me off the move, no matter how cheaply we may have been able to acquire him.

Not that money would have been an object for Jim. He had provided significant investment in the playing staff and had shown similar commitment in upgrading our facilities. I had that desire to really take advantage of our attendances which were increasing naturally with the promotion and entertaining brand of football, and implement the ideas from Baltimore.

We had new dressing rooms put in and built an office block behind one of the stands, a section which Jim rented out to the BBC. The rent we received helped to pay for the cost of the building—a business decision I'm sure he'd thought about beforehand. Then he suffered a heart attack which meant that he had to spend a considerable time away.

I was keen for the stadium to be one that supporters enjoyed coming to and on one walk around I was disgusted with the state of the toilets and so I arranged for them to be upgraded and replaced with facilities that were accommodating and pleasant to use.

They cost £25,000. I remember Jim's reaction when he found out.

"HOW much?!"

I wanted everything to be top class. On the field, off the field. Our conduct as professionals, the facilities for our supporters. I would even have regular meetings with the Club program sellers, turnstile operators and stewards to discuss improvements in service. Far from seeing it as monitoring their performance, these part-time workers welcomed the interaction as it made them feel more involved. As they were. As it should be.

We were unable to hold on to sixth place but when we went through our rough patch, as most teams invariably do, we had already determined our safety and ensured we wouldn't be caught in any relegation struggle. Four losses from five games heading into the last game of the season didn't hurt as much as it might.

The year had been tremendous vindication in that belief we'd tried to cultivate not only in our younger players but for those older heads too, in particular, McLintock with a point to prove to Arsenal for allowing him to leave; what a way to do it. Francis was now getting the recognition he deserved. Even Dave Thomas, who had been questioned by Leeds manager Don Revie over the injury, was performing magnificently.

We drew our last game at Arsenal. It was a credible 1-1 draw but also tremendously important as it meant we finished as the highest placed London club in the league.

That honor hadn't even been something I had contemplated at the beginning of the season but the press began to mention it as a possibility and of course the prospect was seen as a huge achievement. I had unofficially promised the players a bonus of £100 each which would come from my own pocket if they could do it.

After the game at Highbury, Terry Mancini approached the chairman, under the impression that he had been involved in the bonus.

"Cheers for the money, Jim!"

Jim was none too pleased about that, and it was nothing to do with money, but more, I think he was aggrieved that he hadn't been the one to make the gesture. I can look at that event and now with the benefit of hindsight understand that was something which contributed to the breakdown of the relationship between chairman and manager.

It was a season of tremendous achievement for the club and the players and I suppose that was the reason that when Sir Alf Ramsey was sacked from his position as manager of England, I was given the honor of being considered as his successor by the FA committee.

I had to fly up to a restaurant in Glasgow, Scotland, all incognito, to meet the FA committee for an interview. I believe the decision was between Bobby Robson, who was doing excellent work with Ipswich Town, and myself. Bobby and I had known each other from our days together at Fulham and kept in touch; but then Don Revie put his name into the hat and from that point there was only one winner, due to Revie's exceptional reputation for what he'd achieved with Leeds United.

Honestly, I wasn't totally convinced I wanted the job. Bobby, funnily enough, told me afterwards he felt the same way himself. I was proud of my achievement at Queens Park Rangers but going from club management to international team management to a small number of games and a short space of time with your players was not something that appealed to me.

June expressed her concern about it. She thought I was too young and too inexperienced at the highest level to take such a high pressure job. The press could get personal with you if you were in that job and I knew I wasn't ready for that kind of attention. I figured that, should things go well enough, I would still be young enough to be considered again for the post even after two more World Cups. Strangely enough, it was a fairly easy decision to make, though I confess that I think Bobby's greater experience would have made him favorite after Don.

Yet there was some lobbying in the press for me to get the job. David Miller at the *Daily Express* newspaper wrote an article that got a lot of attention suggesting that I and Ron Greenwood team up, with my role being that of the more conventional team manager or coach and Ron working in an advisory capacity. Ron's experience, it was argued, would complement my own ability, particularly in matters of bureaucracy.

Miller suggested two heads may be better than one but insisted that I should be the manager because of my experience abroad and because, in his words, I understood that "professional football exists only because of the people prepared to pay to watch it."

In the end, the Football Association went for experience, not in Greenwood, but Revie. The Leeds manager had previously given every indication that he would spend the rest of his career at Elland Road when he rebuffed advance from Real Madrid after their boss Miguel Munoz resigned in January, and I was stunned to read reports that in the wake of that rejection, I was being considered as the next boss by Santiago Bernabeu himself! Munoz had overseen that most tremendously successful of periods where they won five European Cups in addition to a multitude of other honors. The mere thought that I was being considered to succeed him was an honor of its own.

I never heard anything about that and I'm not sure how true the speculation was as Jim Gregory never spoke about it, but it was tremendously flattering to read it in the press. Queens Park Rangers were flying so high that they may well have been playing against Real Madrid the following year in Europe.

We didn't quite get that far but it was a time that we were so in demand that we had to politely decline the opportunity to be featured on "*Match of the Day.*" Our Football Association Cup match had been shown on the

BBC the previous week and, as I explained to reporter Steve Curry, I did not feel it was in the best interests of the club or the game for us to be featured two weeks running.

"There is a danger in saturation in respect of match coverage," I had said. Little did I know! The point remained that Rangers were in demand. And it was those thoughts of leading them into continental competition that I carried with me when I began to prepare for our second season in the top flight.

nine

The Saddest Day of My Soccer Life

I SHOULD HAVE been looking forward to building on our fabulous first season in Division One, but instead, one Friday late in September 1974, I found myself packing a number of personal items into my shoulder bag and walking out of my office at Loftus Road. It was an end to my four-year association with Queens Park Rangers after a journey which had seen the club promoted to the First Division, a number of our players selected for their country and me even being considered for the national job. What a time.

I left behind a message for the Club secretary, Ron Phillips, to pass on to Jim Gregory that I was resigning from my position effective from that day and I would not be reachable by the media for that weekend. I said that Jim could make any statement to the press that he wished.

I was walking away from the best years of my soccer life, my career, from a superb group of players and a first class staff that had together gained promotion and enjoyed the award from *The Sun* as the "Most Entertaining Team In The Football League."

So where did everything go so wrong?

Every day was a joy to coach the players. Every one of the most prominent twelve players in the squad gained international recognition during my spell at the club. The team I had inherited were flirting so intently with relegation that they seemed hell-bent on making it a serious relationship, yet we won ten of our remaining twenty games of the season to not only move away from an relegation concerns but give us optimism for the following year. It was an optimism well founded as we looked certain for promotion until the Rodney Marsh episode unraveled.

I will never forget the pitch invasion when we finally did clinch promotion the following season, in our last home game. The joy being shown by the supporters was shared by all of us at the club and even though it was a time where the hooligan problem was beginning to plague the English game, this occasion was one of pure celebration.

It all seemed to have happened so quickly. And for me, it had been such an enjoyable experience. Building a team with excellent new players, adding them to the exciting young talent already at the club whose development was such that it wasn't long before we could see we had the makings of a truly first class team.

Not to labor the point, but our first season in the top division saw that progress continue if a little slower than anticipated. Victories that were just as important in the entire history of the club, let alone the single season, over Chelsea, Arsenal and Tottenham Hotspur saw us finish in a very respectable eighth position. We were the premier London club.

We had been confident and yet still surpassed the greatest of our expectations. The atmosphere amongst the players and the supporters was wonderful and I had a quiet but resolute confidence that there was still so much more left for this group of players to accomplish. Qualification for a European club competition seemed a real possibility in the very near future and perhaps—*perhaps*—even some success in the Football Association Cup or Football League Cup.

That was how I felt at season's end in May 1974.

And just five months later I was walking away from that very thing that all soccer managers work for. Success.

So, where *did* everything go so wrong?

Let us be clear. My decision on 27th September 1974 was not a hasty one. I had been awake until the early hours of that morning discussing and procrastinating over every aspect of the decision with my wife. In the end, I knew it was the right decision.

No, the *only* decision.

For all of my life, I had lived by the motto "life is short and should be enjoyed." I could never work in a situation that was an unhappy one. Not that every moment had to be rosy, of course, there will always be times of sadness, or disappointment, and sometimes even unpleasantness, but when those moments become the rule rather than the exception then you have to reevaluate your position. Due to the actions of the chairman, I was no long enjoying my role at the club.

Going back to when I first joined the club, all the way back in 1970. I was continuously asked by many people within the game, "How do you get on with Jim Gregory?" His reputation clearly preceded him. He had the notoriety of apparently being difficult with his club managers and this became very evident once news of my resignation became known.

Jim was a character and not always for the best reasons. He once knocked out a *Sunday People* newspaper reporter, Mike Langley, in the toilets at the Football Writer's awards dinner. The worst possible place! Langley was drunk and approached Jim in the toilet.

"You shouldn't have sold Rodney Marsh."

Jim responded to Langley with some insult. The reporter puts his fists up, Jim goes straight in and hits him, knocking him to the floor.

The next morning Jim calls me and says, "No doubt you've heard about last night."

"Jim, you're the chairman of a big club, you shouldn't belittle yourself."

I told him off, but all the other chairmen called him up to congratulate him!

During my spell of seven months as club coach I had seen examples of how Jim had influenced our then manager, Les Allen, when it came to things like purchasing players, player discipline, team selection and especially player contracts. These were major parts of a manager's responsibility and many times Jim's involvement would not necessarily be to the support of Les or the action he thought ought to be taken.

So, with that in mind, when I accepted the role as caretaker manager, I asked Jim to establish exactly what the ground rules were, so to speak. I wished to know where my role as manager would end and his role as chairman would begin, and ensure there were no grey areas in between.

There were a few things I wanted to establish. I asked Jim that if a player went to his office without speaking to me, he would call me by phone in front of the player and inform me that the player was there. I understood that when Les had been in charge this kind of situation had been common practice, particularly if a player wasn't happy with his contract or had been disciplined by the manager.

Secondly, I said that if I had been instructed to negotiate a contract salary with a player, he would not then renegotiate afterwards, thus undermining me. Thirdly, if the player had a gambling problem, I did not want Jim to be giving him money if I had already refused.

I understood that it would mean a change for Jim. I knew he liked to be around the senior players to socialize and to basically be "one of the lads."

He agreed to my request and all went smoothly in the first eighteen months of our working relationship. The manner in which he dealt with the transfer of Rodney Marsh to Manchester City really was first class and to obtain £200,000 was an illustration of his shrewd business ability. His refusal to budge from the asking price was great because firstly it worked and secondly it showed he had the club's best interests at heart. His instructions that we would not attempt to purchase any new players for a while afterwards were also wise and showed acumen.

The first sign of concern for me occurred when our chief scout, Derek Healy, informed me of a player at Scunthorpe United who we should pursue. This was Kevin Keegan, an outstanding prospect, and available for just £30,000. I called Jim to inform him of the recommendation, because we were playing away, and Scunthorpe were coincidentally playing a local side, Brentford, Jim said he would go along to that game to take a look at the player.

I called Jim on Sunday morning after the game for his assessment and he told me that "Keegan was only a Third Division Player" and he did not wish for us to proceed with any further enquiries. A week later, Liverpool manager Bill Shankly signed Keegan for £30,000. You should know what happened next. He became one of the best center forwards in world football.

To be fair, in our next away game, Jim was travelling with us, and he quietly said to me, "I was wrong about Keegan." I was diplomatic in my response for there was nothing to gain at this juncture.

"We all make mistakes," I reassured him.

Yet I should have been more wary. It was a warning sign I did not pay sufficient attention to because it became very clear over the next few months that if Jim did not take a fancy to a player recommended by Derek or myself, he would find a way to cancel proceedings and end our interest in him.

On one occasion we were looking to sign a young center half and so I met with Glen Keeley of Ipswich Town. The talk went well but Glen remained unsure so said he wanted to return to Ipswich to discuss the move to London with his girlfriend, promising to give me his answer the next morning. I felt that was fine, I came away from our discussion feeling confident that he would join us.

I told Jim, and his response was that because Keeley hadn't accepted our offer there and then, the transfer was off, and the money to purchase him was no longer available. I had the unenviable and extremely unpleasant task of calling the lad the following morning to tell him that our offer was no longer available. I wished him continued success. Short but not so sweet, but at least Glen did go on to have a good career.

The complications around the Don Givens transfer further raised my concern. His initial refusal to pay £40,000 for a player who was certainly worth it was worrying but I was left in a helpless position when he demanded the telephone number of Luton Town manager Harry Haslem. I knew what Jim was going to do and knew that Harry wouldn't stand for it but it was Jim's club, the club's money and therefore his decision. To say I gave him the number reluctantly would be an understatement.

Jim called me two hours later to say he had got Don for £38,000. The glee in his voice was tangible because he had been the one to "get a deal." I felt we were lucky to be getting him at £40,000, and given the jeopardy which Jim caused to the transfer by getting involved, I heighten that description to say we were the luckiest club in the world to get him. Jim was so fortunate that Harry had already gone on holiday to Spain, as Harry confirmed later when he spoke with me to say Luton would never do business with Jim again.

I do not believe Jim wanted us to sign Don Givens and perhaps his intention was to sabotage the deal but he got a better price and so was able to say "I got a better deal than you." He got his satisfaction that way. Jim could feel content in the knowledge that we had already discussed Stan Bowles some time before we begun negotiations and of course everything in the Dave Thomas transfer was initiated by him.

From these experiences I learned that Jim Gregory must like any player you recommended in order for him to be signed to the club, and that Jim wanted to negotiate the transfer fee, if those two elements were not in place, the deal would not be either.

Once I knew the rules, I was okay with that. I was able to continue my work in that environment. Of course, this was helped by the fact that we were successful on the pitch.

As I previously, but briefly, mentioned, Jim Gregory suffered a heart attack during the 1973/74 season and was not allowed to attend games by order of his doctors. It was of course a shame for him that to be the case considering that to his credit his re-investment of the Marsh money had helped us get promoted. For most of that season, our first in the top division, the club secretary Ron Phillips handled all the business aspects, with I and the coaching staff looking after the soccer side of it.

All was rosy, and then, just before the end of the season, Jim returned to work. From then on, our working relationship was very different. As you would expect from a newly promoted team surpassing all expectations, particularly due to the way we were playing, we were enjoying a lot of praise from the media. I was part of that and my reputation was benefitting accordingly. In April 1974 I was approached by Sir Alf Ramsey to coach the England Under 23 side on a three-game summer tour in Europe. It was a request and one I felt an honor, particularly after coaching the National U-18 side previously.

It shouldn't have been a problem aside from the clash that it had with a first team tour of Jamaica which we had arranged as a reward to the players after such a successful year. The opportunity to spend some time sunning themselves on the Caribbean beaches seemed like a just reward. When I tried to explain the situation to Jim, he insisted that I should be with the team in Jamaica and turn down the request from Sir Alf. I was an employee of Queens Park Rangers and that was my responsibility.

Regrettably, I had to contact Sir Alf and notify him of the club's decision. Two days after doing so, Jim asked me to meet him at his office, where he informed me he didn't want me to go to Jamaica after all, and Frank Sibley, our coach, would assume the responsibility. But far from this being a conversation where he was relenting and changing his mind, he said that my job was to remain in England in case the opportunity to sign a new player should arise. This would have made a little sense if not for a phone call I received shortly afterwards, this time from Jim's son, to tell me that his father was going on holiday and there would not be any money available to purchase any new players.

I got the distinct impression that Jim was trying to let me know who was boss and that all of the publicity and praise that I had enjoyed counted for nothing. No, actually, if I'm honest, it felt more serious, more personal, than that. With the final development, the phone call from Jim's son, it became clear that the chairman wanted me to leave. I don't know why he felt that way, but it was certain that was what he wanted, and I wasn't about to outstay my welcome. If that's how Jim felt, then I felt the same way.

I sent a message to him that I was giving him a month's notice, knowing full well that if that notice was accepted, I was essentially gone immediately. Naturally, once the press became aware of the situation, they made a great deal out of it and Jim was forced to publicly deny that he wanted me out. He implied to the press that he thought my letter of resignation was arriving because I'd been offered the England job. I think he knew better.

I received a message from Ron Phillips that said Jim wanted to see me on his return. In this meeting, Jim said he didn't want me to leave and asked me to reconsider. It wasn't an easy decision I'd made to hand in my notice and I'd done so with the expectation that Jim wanted me gone, so with his re-assurance, however tenuous, I agreed to stay. Of course I didn't *want* to leave. He followed that up by saying he'd agreed a deal to sign Dave Webb from Chelsea and asked if that was okay with me. We had previously decided that we would sign a young center half in the mold of Glenn Keeley in order to develop under the tutelage of Frank McLintock so it took me by surprise that we were signing a 28-year-old defender. "Okay," was all I could think to say.

Going back was a disaster. The worst decision I could have made. We got off to a difficult start to the season—no excuses, but it sometimes can be tough in the second year for promoted teams—and then at board meetings,

Jim began to question every move I made and every comment that was said. It was a clear show of strength to demonstrate to me and the board members that he was the one in charge and I was to answer to him.

I remember him asking about the expenditure on the toilets and "HOW much?!" being the reply. I explained the toilets were disgraceful. We were charging the highest price for tickets in the league and we had pig troughs for toilets.

"Why did we purchase a third color strip?"

"So that we didn't have any conflicts if our colors clashed with an opponent."

"Why are we going to Manchester on Friday instead of Saturday morning?"

"For some players who live out of inner London suburbs, to get to Euston Station by 10 am means they might have to get up at 6 am. I don't consider that the best preparation for a First Division league game."

That was the last question at the board meeting on the 26th of September 1974, two days before we were playing Manchester City.

I couldn't tolerate it any longer and decided that for whatever reason, Jim had "won" and I would join the long list of those who could call themselves an ex-Queens Park Ranger manager.

The joy of those early years was now well and truly over.

The 27th of September, 1974 was the saddest day of my soccer career.

ten

Plans of Mice and Men in the Lions Den

"GORDON, I'VE BEEN speaking to the new chairman of Millwall, Mr. Hubert Burnige, and he would like for you to call him."

It's funny how phone calls from Brian Moore seemed to have an impact on my life.

I had been out of work for two or three weeks after leaving Queens Park Rangers but fortunately I had no shortage of offers. That's a manager's lot in soccer. One month you can be seriously considered for the national job, the next, you're out of work. I still don't regret not being selected for the England job and I didn't regret it then. My thought remained that I would still be young enough to be considered if I did well enough at club level by the time the position came around again.

I could confess that I wasn't quite ready for a role of that magnitude with the various pressures and intrusions which were promised to accompany it but I also wasn't quite ready to take a step back. Ron Greenwood, the West Ham manager, had invited me to join him and John Lyall until I found a permanent appointment with a new club.

That was typical of Ron. Anytime a manager lost his position, he would be in touch to offer tickets to a West Ham game. Alex Stock, the former Queens Park Ranger, Luton Town and Fulham manager was cut from the same cloth. Both of them were sheer class acts.

I was considering the invitation from West Ham when Brian called me and so I said I would think about that too.

Having spent twelve years at Charlton, Millwall was our near neighbor and our opinion of them was far from complimentary. They were a team that was well known for hard and tough play, while off the pitch, the supporters were reputedly just as uncompromising, constantly in the news for violent behavior at football grounds around the country.

Fortunately, in my time at the Valley, we were never in the same division as Millwall, but we still had a scheduled fixture against them annually in a charity game for the "Kent County Cup." It was the one time as a player when you did not wish to see your name on the team sheet! You didn't want to spend an afternoon being kicked around and knocked all over the pitch as well as getting verbally abused from the crowd for ninety minutes, and particularly not after a long season!

I deliberated on these thoughts and didn't call the Millwall chairman.

Two days later I received another telephone call from Brian Moore.

"Mr. Burnige would very much like for you to call him," Brian insisted.

Even though I remained unconvinced, I did not wish to be rude and as a matter of courtesy I did make the phone call. To my surprise, I was invited by Mr. Burnige to meet at the Claridges Hotel in Mayfair—one of the most prestigious hotels in London! No disrespect intended but Millwall, Claridges—how did those two go together? I would maybe have only expected a meeting to take place in such a venue if I was being invited to discuss a vacant position at Tottenham Hotspur or Arsenal. However, it wasn't a matter of trying to impress me, simply one of convenience, as I discovered when I got there and saw that Mr. Burnige's office was next door.

Still, the meeting was first class and I left it feeling very impressed indeed with the Millwall chairman. He was straightforward, expressing the serious position of the club both on and off the field. He team was in the bottom three of the league and he was concerned of the increasing problems and reputation of the behavior of the supporters, even though he stressed it was confined to a small percentage of the total who attended. He was honest, saying that funds for new players were scarce, the club was in some debt, but he would do all that was possible to support me with regard to new players and I would have complete control of all playing matters.

The cards were on the table and Mr. Burnige did not pull any punches; he was completely honest and although it was certainly a challenge, I was impressed by the way he conducted our meeting. He felt like a person I could work for and so I accepted his offer, which as a salary, but no contract. Putting aside the fact it was Millwall, from the outside, it seemed to be similar to the situation I'd took over at Queens Park Rangers.

One might say he was more forthcoming than I was. He was obviously very keen to hire me, but my plan was simply to work until the end of the season doing the best I could to implement the changes that the chairman wished to see. Improve the team's performance, avoid relegation, and do what I could to improve the image of the club in the perception of others; and then move on.

Millwall were struggling in the league but had been close to promotion a couple of times so there was obviously some quality in the squad. It was very evident from my first few days in charge that many of the senior players, who had played together for many years, were so disappointed in that failure to gain promotion that they were now looking for new challenges instead. Many of them were already on the transfer list. It didn't make for the best atmosphere and it was a possible reason for the underperformance that year. I could understand and sympathize. It was the exact situation I had feared would happen at Queens Park Rangers.

I thought that the squad would benefit from extra training sessions so informed them that we would be doing so on three afternoons each week. The purpose was nothing to do with fitness, but to improve our organization, both defensively and offensively. I wanted to get our set-piece routines working effectively as I felt they were vital to assisting a teams' performance. That word, organization. The team was lacking structure, perhaps a feeling of restlessness that was a consequence of their previous disappointment.

The immediate reaction was not most pleasing.

"I do schoolboy coaching."

"I have a greengrocery shop I need to be at."

"I have to be home to take care of the children while my wife is out."

And those were the best excuses. Others simply admitted they wanted to have the afternoons free.

The fact that these men were employed as FULL TIME professional footballers was not mentioned but seemed to be lost on them.

The commitment that should have been there didn't seem to be. And when that is the case then was it any wonder that they were struggling as they were? It was such a different attitude to that which I'd experienced from the Queens Park Rangers players. They were players who wanted to improve their individual skills so much that they stayed behind in training even when they weren't instructed to. Their desire to be the very best that they could be was insatiable and contagious. When we had gone to Norway I remember Bobby and I being held back for some reason before training. When we got out to join the players, they were already working in small groups on control and passing. We just stood and watched, observing that marvelous attitude.

And then I get to Millwall and see the complete opposite. I had been prepared for a certain lack of organization but not this, and it got even worse when I discovered the players didn't even have their own individual training equipment or clothes. The trainer would just put out a huge pile of shirts, shorts and socks in the dressing room, all freshly washed, but thrown together, and each player just took the items that he wanted. To me this was not correct, so I ordered all new equipment, including top-class tracksuits. I didn't want Millwall to be seen as the poor neighbors. I wanted them to have class. They didn't even have sit down toilets in many areas of the stadium and there was only one bath in the room for the referees!

However, that attempt was not received by the players as the improvement I would have hoped that they would think. Years later, Gordon Hill, in his book "Merlin," would describe my actions as flashy and against Millwall's identity. He confirmed my suspicions about the resistance I was feeling, saying that I "couldn't change them" as people. That wasn't my intention. I would never neglect my responsibility to the development of young men but seasoned professionals, well, you just have to hope that they share your attitude towards learning and improvement. That did not appear to be the case and it didn't produce the right atmosphere for a team battling relegation.

When faced with a situation like that your options are limited, particularly when as a manager you do not have the funds to regenerate and rejuvenate the squad. I was forced to go against my instinct, an instinct that had proven to be correct when I was at Queens Park Rangers, because the experienced players at Millwall were not committed to the cause.

So, after attempts to try and get some of the players to change their mind and stay, I decided to give some of them what they wanted, and transferred them—Brian Clark went to Cardiff, Doug Allder to Leyton Orient, Gordon Borland to Boston United and Alf Wood to Hull City.

I knew those outgoing players would free up funds to bring some in and I went back to my old club Queens Park Rangers to sign Tony Hazell for £40,000. Jon Moore of Bristol Rovers, Barry Salvage of Brentford, Ray Evans from Tottenham, Phil Summerill of Birmingham City and Ray Goddard, Barrie Fairbrother and Terry Brisley from Leyton Orient all followed. I agreed short term loans for Tommy Baldwin of Chelsea, Ron Davies of Southampton, Dennis Burnett of Hull City and Mike Dillon of Spurs. Twelve players in all. It gives you an idea of the kind of overhaul which was required.

Hazell had an impact on his debut, scoring with a wonderful long distance free kick, and Jon Moore got the other on the day in a 2-1 win over Sheffield Wednesday. It was a welcome win. The first since I had been appointed manager eight games previous, but was the only victory we had in fifteen games.

There was a brief run of good form in January and early February where we won three and drew one from five games. Summerill scored five goals in two of those matches, but just as influential was another loan-signing. Wilf Smith. Sadly I couldn't persuade Wilf to join us on a permanent basis but our subsequent demise was not simply down to that.

Maybe those changes were necessary but I think I made too many. The league table certainly seemed to suggest as much, as we finished in twentieth position. With the recent change in rules to add an extra relegation place, that meant we were relegated to Division Three.

I didn't think that I had anything in terms of quality and that meant I was often acting against my better, measured judgment. Ron Davies had played for Manchester United and so I thought he would be good enough to come in. The consideration of how we might play him or how I might build a team was a secondary issue to trying to work this huge turnaround of players. Players who were known quantities and proven elsewhere but taking players simply on their reputation was at odds with my general philosophy.

I needed more time. I tried to do too much, too soon. I tried to rectify too many problems with one fell swoop.

I had put a great deal of effort in and I had failed. That effort extended beyond the training pitch and playing. I had attempted to instigate the change in perception that Mr. Burnige was keen to see and for the entirety of the first season I was there. I was working twelve to fourteen hours a day, travelling from my home in Richmond across London to Millwall. If I wasn't training I was scouting games in the evenings. If I wasn't doing that, I was visiting local working men's clubs and youth clubs in an effort to improve the relations and reputation of the club.

In my program notes for the final game of the season—a 1-1 draw with Bristol Rovers—I wrote "My pride is hurt for I have failed to steer our club to safety but this is only a temporary failure. It is not really the end, it's really the beginning."

The England U18 Youth team on its European Tour and in Nice, France. Captain Gordon Jago is in the front row with his hand on the ball.

The Lord Mayor of London greeting Captain Gordon Jago of the London School boys team prior to their games against the Glasgow School boys team at West Ham United FC in 1948.

(*Above*) Gordon Jago (fifth from left) at the beginning of his coaching career at North Heath School in 1954.

(*Right*) Gordon Jago at Charlton in 1954.

Watching the coin toss before the England Youth Under 18 versus the Belgium Youth Under 18 teams in Nice, France, 1950.

Gordon Jago (no. 5) in action against Cardiff City during the 1957/58 season

A Charlton photo in August 1957. (left to right) F. Lucas, Gordon Jago, and Billy Kiemann

Charlton versus Rotherham on December 19, 1959 with Gordon in control of the ball.

(*Above*) The Baltimore Bays arrive in Jamaica for preseason training in 1968. (left to right) trainer Al Bataglio, general manager Clive Toye, assistant coach Dennis Viollet, and Gordon Jago.

(*Right*) Charlton Athletic players (left to right, back row) Stuart Leary, Gordon Hearst, Johnny Summers, John Sewell (in front right, Sammy Lawrie) help celebrate the wedding of June and Gordon Jago, March 7, 1960.

The Baltimore Bays on their Jamaican tour in 1968.

(*Above*) A team photo of the Queens Park Rangers for the 1971/72 season.

(*Right*) Gordon Jago with assistant coach Bobby Campbell at QPR discussing tactics in 1972.

eleven

All Smiles at Millwall FC, and the Biggest Mistake of My Life

ONLY TIME WOULD tell if my words ahead of that last game would prove to be right, and it was far from certain that I would still be Millwall manager.

As usual, June had a huge say. She went for my conscience and she was right to.

"You owe it to Mr. Burnige to stay with the club, you don't just walk away because you've been relegated to Division Three," she ordered. It gave me an extra determination to stay.

Every new manager needs time and that is particularly the case at struggling clubs. How often do you see managers get jobs at clubs that aren't struggling (respective to their own expectations of course)? I think Tony Pulis in the modern game provides a wonderful example of how to go into struggling clubs and turn it around. Maybe, now, with the benefit of such a strong reputation, players buy into his ideas quicker, but you still have to do the work and he is rightly revered for the jobs he did notably at Stoke City and Crystal Palace.

I had given myself until the end of the 74/75 season at Millwall and there were too many problems to resolve as quickly as I tried. Relegation may have been inevitable anyway due to the attitude of the players. I honestly believed in my ability to get them out of trouble, but maybe with the thought that I wouldn't be around for a considered amount of time, I was making more impulsive decisions. Decisions which needed to be made, but, taken without the care and considerations with which I normally prided myself on.

So, now I was staying to try and turn it all around, I decided to do that, to begin to make those changes. While I was planning to build the team, I dedicated more time in the off-season to improving the facilities. Retiling the toilets and changing rooms, putting showers in the referee's room. I asked the maintenance man for a new toilet brush; he made good on the request, but when I went in to the bathroom, the brush was in an old paint can! It was farcical. Only a little thing but that was the mentality there.

We had volunteers in everywhere. We worked with the supporter's clubs and they were painting everything. The whole place needed upgrading. Eventually, with that communal pull, things began to turn around, but for those first few months, it seemed like everyone was happy to live in the 1800s.

Mr. Burnige was keen to build a new youth team and so we concentrated on doing just that. The youth team I inherited was sadly very poor. The club had twelve lads who had been playing in the South Eastern Counties and they just weren't good enough. It wasn't easy letting them all go but it was a decision that had to be taken. I made arrangements to find them amateur clubs or interviews for jobs. Six months later, one of the parents of those boys released came to me and suggested another boy for us to look at. I took that to mean that at least they respected the way we had conducted ourselves.

We had Derek Healy, Ted Buxton and Bob Pearson, our scouts looking for talent and they found some unbelievable prospects. They were so good that we had some issues trying to convince parents to allow them to sign for us, with the likes of West Ham United and other London clubs monitoring them too. We were able to do so, and put together a tremendously exciting young side. We recruited Oscar Fullon—an Argentinean know as Oscar Arce—as a youth coach, who really helped their development. He was fantastic and helped Millwall win the Football Association Youth Cup in 1979.

Andy Nelson, then-Charlton manager had said to me, "Good luck playing your football in the Third Division."

But I was keen to. My pride *had* been hurt, but, as I had said, it was just the beginning.

I have to be honest and confess that even though I had committed myself to Millwall, it didn't stop me from being tempted elsewhere. We made a very mixed start to the season and didn't adapt swimmingly to life in Division Three. We were losing as many games as we were winning and couldn't generate any consistency. With Christmas approaching, thoughts of an instant return to the Second Division were optimistic to say the least.

I like to believe I haven't made too many incorrect decisions in my life but in November 1975 I possibly made the poorest decision of my life. I received a phone call from Kurt Lamm, a good friend, who was also the Secretary of the United States Soccer Federation. He told me that the USSF wanted me to consider the position of the US National Team coach and also the Director of Coaching, a position that the excellent German coach Dietmar Cramer had just vacated. The Federation Committee wanted me to meet them in New York to discuss the matter further and so I decided to take them up on the offer.

I couldn't say that life at Millwall had suddenly become tremendously enjoyable. It was a strain. There was a resistance to my determined and concerted attempts to rejuvenate the profile of the club, and that resistance was seemingly shared by all—public and the press, but, also, some club staff! That arduous task was not helped by our lack of fortune on the pitch. I could take responsibility. It was a team I had put together but there was nothing like the rhythm or style I'd been used to seeing from my Queens Park Rangers players. And the supporters didn't seem keen to help. My attempts to liaise with them seem to fall on deaf ears and the problems that accompanied us at games with the hooligan culture were as bad as they had ever been.

The prospect of managing a national team was very attractive by contrast, especially in view of my hurt pride of the relegation. It was a boost to feel worthy of such a prestigious role.

After giving the matter some thought I decided I would fly over to New York on the Sunday following our Football Association Cup First Round tie with Yeovil Town. I could attend the meeting on Monday, and fly back to London that evening. Theo Foley, my assistant coach, would be the only one to know and would conduct training in my absence. With that all in place, I confirmed arrangements with the USSF and booked the flights and hotel.

Of course, Yeovil went and threw a spanner in the works by taking the game to a replay, which was arranged for the following Tuesday. It meant I had to make a hurried call to Kurt to cancel the meeting and send my apologies to the US Federation.

The replay with Yeovil ended in another draw, and this was in the days before it went to penalties. So, a second replay was scheduled at a neutral ground, Aldershot's Recreation Ground, where we won through 1-0 at the third time of asking.

Kurt had been a regular caller and so we selected a new date of the Monday after the second round tie with Crystal Palace, as the USSF naturally wished to come to a conclusion with their search.

Everything was again arranged. I should have known better, because we went and drew again! The replay was again re-arranged for the Tuesday, but, having already let down the USSF once, I felt I could not cancel the meeting a second time. I departed Heathrow on Sunday morning and was met in New York by Kurt—we met a small number of the committee later that evening, and the full committee the following morning. All went well. They explained the responsibilities and terms and so on, which I found to be very satisfactory. I told them that I would return to London and give them a decision within three days. Of course, I owed it to Mr. Burnige to meet him and discuss the matter, particularly if my decision was to accept the job.

At lunch prior to departing for JFK Airport for my evening flight back, Kurt was informed from his office that due to fog in London, Heathrow Airport was closed and all flights to London had been cancelled.

Without a doubt, it was the biggest shock I had ever experienced in my life at that point and, probably, that feeling remains. It was a living nightmare. I would not be back to join the team who were about to play a crucial game in the Football Association Cup—a manager, absent from his duty because he had flown thousands of miles to consider another position.

I could envisage the headlines in the newspaper.

It was a disgrace that I do not believe I could have lived with.

How would any club consider me for another managerial role or even one as a coach? I was certain to lose my job, and it was a matter of which came first, instant dismissal or my resignation to try and save face.

I rushed to the airport anyway in a panic to see what I could do. Of course, you can imagine the scene at the terminal. I was not alone. Long lines of passengers attempting to rebook with the airline staff not knowing when to advise on Heathrow being open or if and when the next flights would even take off.

I searched for a representative of the airline and was fortunate to find a gentleman who like football. I told him of my major problem and asked if there were any flights going anywhere in the UK. He said there were flights into Manchester and Glasgow but both were full. To this day I do not know how he found a seat for me on the Manchester-bound flight but he did, after a rush across the terminal and through immigration. I am not exaggerating when I say I had literally just taken my seat on the plane when it began to taxi out on to the runway.

Transatlantic flights usually present a welcome opportunity to sleep and I would normally do so with ease but that was not going to happen this time around. After all, I had only cleared one part of the problem. Would I be able to get a train from Manchester into London, would I get to Crystal Palace Football Club in time for kick off?

I must have annoyed the poor flight attendant, badgering her for information as I was, about how to get to Manchester Piccadilly Station from the airport and how long it might take to get to Euston London from there. She was a great help and I was able to make it to Piccadilly Station in time to catch a train to London. Before I boarded, I made a quick call to Theo, bringing him up to date and informing him that I hoped to meet him and the team at the ground.

Time was still on short supply as I arrived at Euston Station, though I was able to get a taxi to take me to my home in Richmond, have him wait while I dropped off my luggage and quickly changed, before going to Selhurst Park Crystal Palace Ground. I arrived there at 5:45 pm—fifteen minutes before the team did, in preparation for the 7:30 pm kick off.

"Hi boss!" says Barry Kitchener, one of the first to enter, "You look tired!"

He didn't know the half of it, the thirty-six hours of exhaustion and mental pressure I had just endured. It was hard to imagine that Barry, club captain and Millwall through and through, would understand why I'd done what I did. I wasn't sure that I did.

We lost 2-1 and were knocked out of the Football Association Cup.

Two days later, I received telephone calls from Phil Woosnam, the former West Ham United player and Welsh international who at the time was Commissioner of the North American Soccer League, and also Clive Toye, the former *Daily Express* journalist who was the General Manager of the New York Cosmos. Their advice was identical.

"Do not take the US National Team Coach position."

They explained that Dietmar Cramer had resigned because of great difficulties of the position at the time, not least, the lack of American players who were good enough for international competition. They felt that it was a position that was destined to fail or be fraught with difficulties. It was advice that I knew I had to take, because neither of them would have gone out of their way to make those calls if they thought I may have been doing the right thing.

So, I contacted Kurt Lamm and explained my decision, giving them my thanks for their consideration and also patience. The sorry episode is briefly mentioned simply as an "unscheduled trip to the USA" in James Murray's book, "Millwall—Lions of the South." It is documented as though I went on holiday as an emotional reaction to the draw with Yeovil. The book reports me as being emotional and shaking after that game because I was so disappointed and that is the truth.

I will also be grateful to Theo Foley for covering for me in that difficult time, and, to this day, until this book goes into print, there are only a few people aware of my terrible decision. I'm not sure any of them—the airline employee, the flight attendant, the taxi driver—are aware of how important "getting me to the game on time" was to my career.

The incredible weekend and the nearness of my disgrace as a Football League manager sent me a message. I should concentrate on my task of making Millwall Football Club successful both on and off the field in the same way I'd tried to do at Queens Park Rangers.

I was so fortunate that the rest of the season went like a fairytale, and, like all good fairytales, it had a happy ending. On the 21st of February we suffered a 3-1 defeat to Gillingham that put us in to 10th place in the league. Over the next fifteen games we went on an unbeaten run that included winning ten—it was as close to perfect as we could be. Only once during that run did we concede a goal before half-time and we let in just three more goals, too—an outstanding record of eleven games without conceding a goal.

Still, there were moments where promotion seemed out of reach. Four wins on the run and six out of seven saw us leap up the table to fourth and start to seriously entertain thoughts of promotion. But then we drew four games from five—all of them goalless.

Not the results that we needed and now a doubt in our minds that we could rise up the league table and gain that all important target—promotion back into the Second Division.

Yet again in my soccer career, a telephone call would play an important part in my soccer future.

"You received a call from Romark this morning and he wishes you to call him." The words from our club secretary Gordon Borland as I walked into the office following the morning's training session.

"Romark" and interesting name that had been receiving a great deal of publicity in the London media.

A famous hypnotist and illusionist he had offered his services to Malcolm Allison the former Manchester City manager and now the manager of Crystal Palace to assist in their quest for success in the Football Association Cup semi final and also promotion to the Second Division.

It appears that Romark's offer had been rejected by Allison bringing forth a reply by Romark that he had put a curse on Crystal Palace and they would not enjoy the success that they desired at that time!

We learned later that "Romark" had suffered a stroke some months previously and he was struggling to continue his "Stage Profession."

The episode was an attempt by him to obtain media coverage and put his name back into the public eye. Thus this rather outlandish statement.

My first reaction to "Romark's" request to return his call was to ignore it but then not to be rude I decided to call him. A pleasant conversation between us and a further request from him for us to meet. My thoughts at that time was that I really had more important things to do with my time but again I relented and agreed to meet with him.

The subject of the meeting became "our gaining of promotion." Romark stated he could hypnotize our players and give them thoughts of confidence that they would take into their games and assist their performances!

I really did not have an immediate reply for it would be stepping into a zone that I did not have any knowledge whatsoever. I told him I would discuss his offer with our players and it would be their decision to accept or reject.

I believe I made that decision because during that recent run of drawn games a few of the younger players had shown signs of the pressure and perhaps a loss of confidence. This was proved to be somewhat correct when at the player's meeting with Romark six players stated that they would be prepared to join him in his proposal, for him to hypnotize them a day before a game.

If I had been asked before the meeting to name the players most likely to accept I would have named five of the six so my previous thought of pressure and confidence were possibly correct.

I agreed to allow this "experiment" before our next home game against Halifax Town on one condition—all conversations and actions between Romark and each player would remain between them. There would not be any public comment whatsoever by Romark or the players.

Following training on Friday morning each one of the players who had requested Romark's services met with him privately in the director's board room. Other than knowing that he had hypnotized each player that was all one was aware of.

Saturday afternoon's game against Halifax Town was almost a disaster. We won 1-0 but we were very fortunate. We did not play well and one young player, Phil Walker, was taking impossible shots on goal from distances of thirty and forty yards.

You can imagine how I felt for I had brought Romark to the players and I had agreed and setup their meetings. It was down to me.

I informed the players after the game that it was a needed win and we would discuss it fully at training on Monday morning. I needed time to think on how to deal with the situation.

I did take Phil aside quietly after the game and asked him why he was taking shots on goal from such long distances. His answer was so interesting.

Romark had told him while hypnotized that he was going to score "a wonder goal" from forty yards! I very seldom swear but on this occasion under my breath I did say a few choice words of what I would do to Romark.

Having Sunday to consider all aspects I decided to question each player separately on Monday morning and then decide a course of action. Although at that time I was going to cancel any further sessions with Romark.

The main points that came from those meetings was that Romark had entered an area that he knew very little—football. Telling Walker that he would score with a long range shot being a perfect example.

It was interesting also for Phil Summerill to tell me that his new born baby had woken him crying and each time he awoke the first thing he thought of were the words spoken at his meeting on Friday morning. Never having an experience of hypnotism it was all new to me.

In spite of my concerns it did appear that the players involved had a certain calm about their experience with Romark and would like to continue the experiment.

There was only one solution. I would meet with Romark and instruct him to continue meeting those players who wished to continue but he was to refrain from any instructions or suggestions of football skills and plays.

Our meeting was short and to the point. He agreed to my instruction and he continued to meet with the six players. The next two games ended in 0-0 ties, so his record was one win, two ties, five points out of a total of eight and most importantly no goals against.

Going into the last three games over the Easter weekend, we knew we had to win them all in order to have the chance of promotion. Our home games against Brighton and Peterborough were straightforward enough as we took command early on in both games and achieved victories, before our trip to Swindon Town on the Tuesday. At Swindon, it took a little longer after a goalless first half but two strikes in the second half, one from John Seasman and one from Phil Summerill, earned us the win. Supporters came on to the pitch joyously celebrating but the fact of the matter was that Crystal Palace still had two games to play even though we had completed our league schedule. A large number of Millwall fans went to Crystal Palace's last game to cheer on the opposition. Crystal Palace had to win their last game to overtake us and for them to gain promotion.

I was called at home by BBC radio towards the end of the game for reaction in case we went up. Then they went off the line and all I could hear was the crowd. June, Kim and I all sat there, and I was listening as nervous as anything. Eventually the BBC representative came back on and said, "It's 1-1, you're up!"

We will never know how much Romark's influence and on the six players individuals performances but there did appear to be a more confident atmosphere displayed.

One action by Romark that did assist us, without a doubt, was that on traveling to the last three away games he spent the time performing "magic tricks." Showing how some worked and some he kept a secret. They were excellent and all of us were fascinated with his skill. For a period on the journeys, we were trying to discover how he performed the tricks, we were not thinking of the game to be played later that day.

I think Romark achieved what he wanted out of his disagreement with Malcolm Allison—Southampton defeated Crystal Palace in the Cup and we beat them to promotion. I'd be lying if I said I didn't enjoy getting one over on Allison, too. There was a great picture of our captain Barry Kitchener smoking a cigar and wearing a hat, mimicking the image of Malcolm at the time.

After some very tough days, I was finally enjoying the game again, and looking forward to the challenge which lay ahead.

twelve

The Darkest Days

I WAS BOLD and ambitious when I declared that should we get promoted from the Third Division then we should aim to get to Division One right away. But I felt it was possible.

"I'm not worried about the Second Division," I told *Evening Standard* newspaper reporter Peter Blackman. "We have so many good youngsters in our side and more on the way up. I'll be telling my staff to stop all the usual talk of consolidating in the Second Division next season. I'm not interested in that. I want an all-out drive on the First Division. I've never been more serious about anything in my life."

It was how I felt but I knew from experience that the effects on morale and mentality could be profound. I knew there was a certain amount of bravado in it; talk is cheap, but can be so effective.

Although I can't say for sure, I do feel that Jim Gregory at Queen's Park Rangers had resented some of the praise I had received for the performance of the team. Such was the impression I had of him from the time we got to know each other, that I'm sure he felt just as responsible in certain aspects. He spent a lot of money, after all, regardless of whether you are of the opinion that the money received in the sale of Rodney Marsh should be reinvested in the squad. He spent the money so perhaps he felt as if he deserved some of the praise that I was receiving. And maybe, returning after some time away from the club, he felt pushed out and wanted to reassert himself.

No matter what the perception or the thoughts of others, the truth was that money had been spent on Bowles, Givens and Thomas. The first two in particular were as sure to be certainties as you could hope for and so the big transfer fees could be known in advance to be worthwhile outlays.

At Millwall, we had gained promotion from the Third Division on a budget that could be described as a shoestring compared to that at Queens Park Rangers. The money we did receive for Gordon Hill had to be reinvested into the club to keep it running and even with a turnover of players, the fees of those I brought in would vary from £10,000 to £40,00.

I knew that we wouldn't suddenly benefit from an injection of cash. We had a loyal supporter base and I remained dedicated to the improvement of our attendances but it wasn't realistic to suggest or hope that the short-term future would present a challenge any different in real terms to that which we'd taken up the previous year—to contend with teams who had bigger budgets and greater expectations. We were still a little short in some areas. I should have signed Chris McGrath after his loan period but I knew we couldn't afford the fee of £30,000.

Still, by and large, we maintained our defensive qualities which had served us so well towards the end of the previous season, and in early September we thumped league leader Chelsea 3-0 to send a huge message to our rivals. Blackpool were our next opponents and they had taken over at the top. We lost there 4-2, but followed that up with four consecutive victories. The last of which helped us on our way to a victory over Bristol Rovers which lifted us to fourth in the table.

It was form we couldn't sustain but we finished a respectable tenth. We were defeated in the League Cup quarter final by Aston Villa just before Christmas and followed that up with a defeat at home to Nottingham Forest when victory would have lifted us into third. Forest went on to be promoted and never looked back. We won just three of our last eleven games of the season with neither relegation to worry about or promotion a truly realistic possibility.

Still, it was progress. We enjoyed some good results, beating second-place Bolton and drawing at first-place Chelsea in consecutive weeks in February. We knew that on "our day" we could compete with anyone and so the ambition for the following campaign was to make "our day" become a regular thing.

Promotion, if it came, would still have to be pursued on a budget but the one thing we had which we didn't have a year before was more of an established position higher in the domestic ladder and that enabled us to attract a better quality player.

I signed Bryan Hamilton, the Everton player. His salary was £120 a week—£20 above our weekly salary cap of £100. I thought it would be disrespectful to our four top earners who had done so well for us, to be earning less and I knew they would find out. So I approached the chairman and said I wanted to raise all of their wages to the same amount as we were offering Hamilton, and that in order to do so, I would find the money by letting one or two of the talented young players we had go. Mr. Burnige said I didn't need to worry—he'd find the money.

I called in Barry Kitchener to inform him about the news and that he would be getting more money. We weren't forcing them to sign a new deal. But I think Barry, and the other three players, were very happy with what we had done. I remembered taking over at the club and the disillusion I'd found in players who had just missed out on promotion. Now, with time under my belt and relationships with the players, I was able to better prepare for a real push to get to Division One.

Or, so I thought.

I was contacted by the BBC at the beginning of the 1977/78 season because they had heard, and seen, about the difference in attitude at Millwall Football Club. Millwall, as I've said, and is no doubt commonly known, long had a reputation of being involved in the "hooligan" culture, but with promotion and my record at Queen's Park Rangers I suppose that it was only natural that more attention was paid to us.

I had prepared for that and of course it was one of my duties, and, one of the wishes of the Chairman, to improve the image of the club. It is important to stress that at the time, the sport of football was in the stranglehold of hooliganism. It was not a problem confined to Millwall. English football was really suffering with the most high-profile or prominent example of hooliganism being in the European Cup Final of 1975 when supporter riots broke out on the terraces of Paris' Parc des Princes stadium in the game between Bayern Munich and Leeds United. I went to see Holland play England and witnessed some appalling behavior. Even Oxford United, from the University City, had its problems.

We brought out an identity card for supporters that enabled them to get cheaper travel tickets for the away games. We would have stewards and police travel with them on the trains with the understanding that if there was any trouble, the cards would be confiscated, and the corresponding benefits suspended.

With a Sunday morning market held at out stadium and all the other things the board and I were doing to try and raise the profile of the club in a positive sense, I was hopeful that it would reflect in the press in that manner. I did receive a little criticism when I proposed (tongue in cheek) changing the name of the uncompromising Cold Blow Lane to "Montego Bay Crescent" with the council. The supporters reacted angrily even though it was a joke, but it was representative of the wider point I was making.

However, with all this in mind, when I was approached by the BBC who suggested they would like to produce a program on our efforts to combat the troubles in the game (at least as far as our club was concerned) then I felt it had to be a positive thing.

The BBC crew came in for three weeks and to say it was a disaster . . . would be kind! We allowed them to come in and do their work but when we were shown the program that they intended to air, we were horrified. They got some supporters drunk in a pub near to the stadium and cajoled them into saying unsavory things about what they were going to do. There were scenes of a hooligan group wearing surgical masks which were apparently part of our support, but we had never seen them before.

The BBC hired a bus to put three hooligan groups together (The "F Troop," the "Half-way Liners" and "Treatment") and take them to Bristol for our away game there at Rovers in early November. The bus broke down, but a passing car picked up two of the biggest lads, who completed their journey. Once on the terraces, they were picking fights wherever they could, and of course, that meant the BBC got plenty of footage.

We tried to get the show pulled and stopped them from airing. However, what made it even worse was that when the attempt failed, we were supposed to be given time after the program to put across our own point of view in response. But there was a "Firemen's" strike at that time which they gave a special news report to.

So, it was shown, in all its glory, manufactured mistruth, giving us no real right of reply.

And just like that, everything we had worked so hard to achieve had been undermined and ruined.

I was so distraught by the events, by the injustice, that I had decided I could no long continue my role as manager.

I had worked for two-and-a-half years, in the longest of days, working night after night to try and promote our efforts to change our image. It killed me. The worst thing was that we knew we were winning the battle. We were succeeding. The hardest part of it all was changing the perception of the public and we were doing just that . . . the show literally killed all of that momentum and returned us, as appropriately described by James Murray in his book "Millwall—Lions of the South," right back to the Dark Ages.

We had a meeting with Dennis Howell, the Minister of Sport and the BBC Chairman Michael Swann. Mr. Burnige, our chairman told them, "I've lost a manager over this. If I could resign, I would."

Dennis Howell described it as an "irresponsible" broadcast and I couldn't agree more. Who in their right mind would go to Millwall after seeing that program? Who in their right mind would take their young children? I've never heard such a stern argument that was conducted without bad language as I did that day. Mr. Howell and Mr. Burnige made their feelings perfectly clear but it was too little, too late. They could do nothing. The producer of the program tried to suggest that he was merely "highlighting" the problem rather than inventing it but Howell argued a very good point that it was likely to encourage violent supporters from other clubs to "seek out" these supposed fan groups and try and achieve similar notoriety. It was creating a potentially huge problem.

It was senseless. Disgraceful.

The BBC seemed to want a sensational story about hooliganism rather than to report the truth. The truth on this occasion was a club trying to better its standing in the community and managing to do that. The real story should have been a heartwarming one. Instead, some sensationalized concoction which played up to stereotypes and ignored everything that was actually going on for good was broadcast, setting not only the reputation of the club, but that of the game, back.

Had I been too sensitive? You could say so. I know that it was said that I was "too nice" to be successful. But it was a matter of integrity and principle. By permitting the BBC to come in, even though I had no idea at all what was about to transpire, I felt I had let the club down. I had been all for it and invited them in to do what they wanted.

Mr. Burnige didn't want me to leave. I had eighteen months remaining on my contract. But I thought there was no way I could face the supporters any longer, that I had let them down as much as anyone.

It hadn't been an easy season on the pitch—it didn't look as if we would push for promotion that year—but I didn't expect things to move as quickly as they had at Queen's Park Rangers. We didn't have as much money and we would have even less with the inevitable drop in attendances I felt was sure to follow. We would eventually be in a position where we could generate money through our youth system but I knew that in the short term at least, in order to maintain our progress on the pitch, it was absolutely crucial to maintain the progress we had made off of it. Once that was gone, we didn't have a Jim Gregory as financier.

We had progressed so far in such a short space of time and in many ways, the very fact that we had done it without any financial assistance, it had all been self-generated, gave us the greatest pride. To go from that satisfaction and the hope of seeing all of that good work shown to the nation, to what transpired, was horrific. It was heart breaking. Soul destroying.

Mr. Burnige died a couple of years after and I felt a terrible guilt that everything that happened contributed in some way. I still do carry that guilt with me even though I am reassured by a good relationship with his son, Jeff.

I felt guilty too about leaving the club in a position which some melodramatically described as a "sinking ship." It was far from that. It could hold its own, not least thanks to the fantastic youth team that was breaking through, and it was a club in far better shape than the one I'd taken over.

I had been on holiday to Tampa the previous summer and was invited as a guest to the Tampa Bay Rowdies. When I was at Queen's Park Rangers in 1974 they had offered me the head coach position but I declined, instead, suggesting other names such as Eddie Firmani, who eventually got the job. Eddie would ask my advice on European players and we kept in touch that way.

When I went over for the vacation, Eddie suddenly left to join the New York Cosmos. It looked bad because the local press began to speculate that I was there to take over and the owner, George Strawbridge, actually did offer me the position. I declined.

They appointed former Chelsea player John Boyle but he departed at the end of that season. The end of his reign coincided with my troubles at Millwall and when George Strawbridge came calling again, I was far more receptive to his advances.

Unbeknown to me at the time, that episode at Millwall would represent my final days as a manager in the English game. In later years I would wonder if it was a flaw in me which caused me to react the way I did and resign both at Millwall and Queen's Park Rangers. Both times, I'd left for reasons that were not to do with the team's performance. The first because of the bad relationship I had with Jim Gregory and the second because of, how *do* you categorize what went on at Millwall? Non-football circumstances?

I felt destroyed. I felt as if I was faced with a challenge that had already defeated me, one I could not turn around.

thirteen

Getting Rowdy

"IF I EVER do get offered the job, and I'm thinking about it, remind me of this day." I can clearly remember telling June at the game in Tampa during our vacation. The temperature must have been a very unpleasant 100 degrees.

And she did, a few times.

Still, I found myself in Tampa in charge of the Rowdies.

It's probably appropriate to at least address the move a little more. I have explained why I left Millwall but that doesn't reveal why I felt it was necessary to relocate thousands of miles away, a decision that could be seen as drastic or even an overreaction.

The circumstances surrounding my resignation at both Queens Park Rangers and Millwall had essentially come down to a matter of principle. Both times I felt as if I had no other option. Sometimes that is harder to live with than it would be, say, if I'd been sacked, or relieved of my duties.

Nevertheless, the principles I stood by in the 1970s, I still stand by today. And I am quite resolute that I could no longer tolerate working with Jim Gregory at Queens Park Rangers. I wasn't enjoying my profession.

But I took what happened at Millwall very personally and so when the Tampa Bay Rowdies opportunity came back around, it was undoubtedly with the influence of how low I was that I made the decision to go. Conventional wisdom would tell you that it is indeed probably not very wise to make such a huge decision based on a temporary emotional moment; fortunately, it turned out to be one of the best decisions I did make.

I was so emotionally and physically drained from the hard work at Millwall, let alone my natural reaction to all of that work having gone to waste, that the move to Florida really represented a sunnier, more fruitful life. A change is as good as a rest, so they say.

Still, as is the case in soccer, Tampa Bay were in need of improvement and that's why they needed a new head coach. I inherited a squad that had some familiar names. Derek Smethurst, the former Chelsea player, and, lo and behold, Rodney Marsh, who had been in town for a couple of years. It seemed like the easiest way to get players was to get them on loan from English clubs and I brought in Jim Fleeting, Mick McGuire and Graham Paddon from Norwich City.

It's funny how your memory of how things happened and how they actually did can seem completely different. At the time, it felt like it took a while to turn things around on the pitch but the records clearly show that the "transitional" period was around four or five months—a relatively short time in which I was seemingly able to get the best out of the players in a fashion that I felt would bring us success. And it did. We went on a remarkable run of good form. We qualified for the playoff's and then just seemed to grow in confidence from that point, defeating Chicago Sting, the San Diego Sockers and our state rivals Fort Lauderdale Strikers to qualify for the 1978 Soccer Bowl against the famous New York Cosmos.

Rodney had been performing to the standard I was familiar with in our first few months together at Queen's Park Rangers. He was outstanding and that form was acknowledged when he was selected for the NASL All-Star team. Against Fort Lauderdale in the semifinal, he scored the decisive score for us in the 35-yard shootout.

During the game, Rodney had picked up an injury. He had suffered a cut on his shin in a challenge and afterwards, it became infected. Mick Maguire, another of our best performers, also suffered an injury.

We went to New York for the NASL final and Rodney still didn't feel right. He was taking antibiotics and anti-inflammatory tablets to try and reduce the swelling and we agreed he would have a fitness test on the morning of the game. Our hotel was opposite Central Park and when the morning came, Rodney, Mickey, our trainer, our doctor and myself all went into the park to test their fitness. Mickey said he'd play for as long as he could, but Rodney said he was not fit to play.

We were surprised. If anything, I felt that Mick wouldn't feel up to it because his injury seemed worse than Rodney's. I wondered if, in fact, there was another reason. There was a lot of British media attending the game and was Marsh concerned that with his injury he wouldn't be at his best, and he didn't want them to judge him too harshly?

New York Cosmos, with Carlos Alberto, Franz Beckenbauer and Giorgio Chinaglia, were overwhelming favorites. Did Rodney feel that he would be overshadowed? The Rodney Marsh I felt I once knew would have relished the opportunity and the stage to outshine them all. Even in defeat, he could have shown that. And even with Rodney, defeat was almost certain. Such was the strength of the Cosmos.

We went two goals behind in the first half but showed tremendous spirit to rally in the second period. Honestly, I did feel that in Rodney's absence, there was something about the attitude amongst the rest of the players that suggested that they weren't too enamored with his antics. Perhaps they felt that under previous management, they saw Rodney get away with a lot and receive special praise. It was not too dissimilar to how I felt some of the younger players had grown to perceive Rodney. Now, with the pressure off, and nothing expected of them but defeat, the players gave it a really good go and got back into the game. Sadly, just three minutes after scoring, we suffered the sucker punch of a third goal, and the Cosmos used their pedigree and experience to see out the game.

Still, I think that our celebrations after the defeat were more enthusiastic than that of the winners.

> "As hard as the team had played that day, their fans and friends partied deep into the night," wrote Tampa Bay sports columnist Mike Tierney. "Fueled by drink and by a sense of accomplishment, they congregated with players in a Manhattan hotel to dance and to sing and to reminisce and gush excitedly about next year. A Cosmos' victory celebration? Hah. The Cosmos has already headed home. These were the Tampa Bay Rowdies who, you had to occasionally remind yourself, lost Soccer Bowl '78 Sunday afternoon 3-1 to the New

> Yorkers at Giants Stadium across the Jersey state line. This raucous revelry was a celebration of second-best. What if, Lord help us, the Rowdies had won? Would this bash have approached the noise level of Times Square on New Year's Eve?
>
> "BUT WE DID win, really. We won just by getting here," shouted the coach, Gordon Jago, between lusty songs. Behind a smile, he kept apologizing for the behavior of his relatives and British acquaintances."

I was later quoted as admitting my boys had performed a "small miracle" to get to the Soccer Bowl, with Tierney adding that we would have needed a medium-sized miracle to get any further, even with Rodney in the side.

The American's attitude to performing in games is decidedly different to the British and Rodney was as bemused as anyone, asking reporters why he was to blame. But Rowdies' fans back home weren't happy with him; some rang *The St. Petersburg Times* newspaper and demanded that Rodney should take a lie detector test.

Of course, I would never have publicly hung Rodney out to dry. I supported his decision not to play because if he was being truthful then of course he shouldn't have. And even if he wasn't, I knew all too well how much it could damage the team to have an unenthusiastic Rodney Marsh in it.

In their victory, Cosmos were immediately tipped as favorites to retain the Soccer Bowl the following year too, such was their spending clout, but I was bullish about that.

"We'll get them next year," I said, as much in hope (or probably more so) than expectation.

In that first year we had surpassed expectations and in that respect I could then at least have some cause to feel my first year had been successful; as, of course, was seemingly reflected in the celebrations of my players.

This was at a time when the NASL was thriving and although, generally, the league's star European players were at the back end of their careers, it wasn't necessarily portrayed as a graveyard for them. Nor did it feel like that for me. I felt reborn and enjoyed a renewed enthusiasm about the game. It took just a couple of games to get caught up in the infectious atmosphere of the Rowdies, who did well to justify their moniker. In 1974, when the

Rowdies were formed, there was no soccer in Tampa, period. So George Strawbridge, coming from Philadelphia, was already taking something of a leap of faith in the unknown. From 1974 to 1978, to be averaging 30,000 people, was a tremendous success.

My familiarity with how things were run in the US game from my time in Baltimore gave me an ease with which I could introduce or help manage similar promotional activities in Tampa. And we were attracting interest from television companies all over the world, who were keen to see what made our atmosphere so unique. In 1980 Jasper Carrott, a well-known British comedian at the time, came over for three weeks to film a Boxing Day (December 26) special.

Nobody could seem to get enough of us and I was the same. I would turn up to games earlier than usual to sample the atmosphere; supporters would be having cook-out competitions in the parking lot prior to matches. There'd be a Dixieland jazz band going around the concourse; a fellow called Crazy George, moving around the stadium and banging a drum to a chorus of "Go Rowdies!"

We attracted many casual supporters that way, who would come to see the off-pitch entertainment and stay for the soccer. The marketing was out of this world; a step above what I'd previously seen. It seemed as if everything they thought of was successful; that in itself is an accomplishment, but to consider that they had come from literally nothing in 1974 to now out-drawing the Tampa Bay Buccaneers in the NFL gives you some indication of how incredibly well they had done.

After how hard I'd tried to get this kind of atmosphere at Millwall, it was pleasing to be within it, and after a year of great success I could really feel as if I had played my own part in it. But I was sincere with the thought of going back and winning the Soccer Bowl the following year because, after all, the aim of the game is to improve each year.

As well as the game had done, there were still profound differences between that and the European game. The NASL was popular because of its showmen and the Rowdies, with Marsh firing on all cylinders, were no different. There wasn't the concentration on youth development. After all, youngsters were only just being introduced into the game on such a major scale. It stood to reason that we needed our star man going forward. It was a big deal for the Rowdies to have Rodney because the star names would usually go to the Cosmos. Make no mistake, on the top of his game, Rodney would have not looked out of place in any Cosmos team. But, with the game as it was, you could also understand the frustration of supporters when he wouldn't play through the pain.

And so, with no young up-and-coming stars ready to step into the space left by Marsh, it stood to reason that the best way to appease the supporters—and prepare for any lingering issues with Rodney down the line—would be to bring in a stellar name to the frontline. Mike Flanagan had enjoyed success with Charlton Athletic but, on a loan spell with the New England Tea Men, he scored thirty goals in 28 games, grabbing the attention of all the NASL teams. His price was reportedly $1.5m but I was keen to get him—so, I identified him as a player I wanted to George and hoped he would be able to conclude a deal. The structure of the game differed on that level and, honestly, that may be a reason why I was enjoying life that much more. I knew nothing of the finances, it was not my responsibility. I was a coach, not a manager. I wasn't charged with transforming fortunes off of the field. I did feel as if I were contributing by hopefully keeping the Rowdies successful and playing entertaining football on it.

Spotting talented players who would improve us was part of that philosophy. I flew to England to try and negotiate the deal for Flanagan but it didn't come off. Rodney's nose had been put out of joint, presumably thinking we were seeking to replace him.

Even if Mike had been of the persuasion to return to the NASL, he may have been tempted to join the strong British contingent at Vancouver Whitecaps. Under Tony Waiters, they were emerging as strong contenders to the Cosmos, with their solidity a powerful match for the star quality in New York. English players Phil Parkes, Roger Kenyon, Ray Lewington, Alan Ball, Trevor Whymark, Scottish star Willie Johnston and future Liverpool legend Bruce Grobbelaar were in their ranks. As good as they were, it was of no concern to us. We were in the American Conference and they, like the Cosmos, were in the National Conference. If we qualified for the play-offs, we would only meet one of them in the final. As confident as we were of being at the Soccer Bowl again, we fully expected that our opponents would be the Cosmos.

We didn't acquire Flanagan but we did sign Oscar Fabbiani, a relatively unknown striker from Argentina who would take to the NASL like a duck to water. The league had just secured a huge television deal with ABC and our regular season game with the Cosmos was selected as the first game to be broadcast live. We won and this showed signs of our progress and gave us hope that we might come out victorious should our paths cross in the Soccer Bowl.

Discontent with those rumors about signing Flanagan, Marsh had knocked on the general manager's door and asked for an improved contract. By this time, however, the player was not as popular with the board as he was with the supporters. I can't speak for anyone else but I would think that Rodney's absence from the Soccer Bowl had been perceived as an easy decision to make and was still rubbing people up the wrong way, despite the player's apparent commitment in the off-season. Yet when the request for a new contract was presented as "pay me more, or trade me," it was an ultimatum not taken favorably by the board, and they called his bluff, feeling that he wouldn't really move as he and his family were settled in the area.

I, myself, had grown a little weary of Rodney's antics. Our general manager Chas Serednesky came out in the press talking of how no player had ever sought to renegotiate their contract before; clearly, the board felt that the player had a lot of making up to do before being rewarded with a new deal. My own stance was pretty straightforward, that I only wanted committed players.

To that end, I did feel that Rodney had showed commitment. He had lost weight and, in showing that he at least wanted a new contract, was demonstrating that he wanted to stay. So I had no issues with playing him and together we enjoyed another successful season, winning the American Conference again and qualifying for and through the play-offs to remarkably make the Soccer Bowl. Vancouver had caused an upset to defeat the Cosmos to qualify themselves and even though they were still the favorites, we were ostensibly in a better position than a year ago.

This time we had no fitness concerns with Rodney and furthermore, it could be argued that our new signing, Fabbiani, had quickly evolved into our best, or at least most important, player of that season. At the very least, we weren't so heavily reliant on Rodney. For once, it wasn't all about him, until he decided to make it so, announcing that he was to retire after the Soccer Bowl.

The club generously awarded him a testimonial for a big send-off—something never before done in the North American game. So, there was the hullabaloo surrounding that, which also now presented the Soccer Bowl as Rodney's last professional game.

I had hoped that the stars would align and Rodney would put on one last show but he was desperately below par. We had done well to recover from an early deficit from a Whymark goal, equalizing through Jan van der Veen midway through the first half, but when Whymark got his second after an hour, it was clear I needed to act in order to give us the best chance. I gave it ten minutes before my first change, replacing Steve Wegerle with Peter Baralic, and sending Peter on with the word that I would soon be taking Rodney off, and prepare the team for a slightly altered, more offensive shape. When Rodney heard, he looked right at me. If looks could kill.

The next time he received the ball, he went on a mazy dribble, beating three or four players in that way that Rodney could. He put in an effort on goal that was desperately close, destined for the top corner until the goalkeeper pulled off a great save. Rodney then looked over at me as if to say, "That's what I can do." That was all well and good, but he wasn't doing it. It had taken the acknowledgement of his imminent withdrawal to provoke him into life.

I wasn't convinced, and brought him off for Ivica Grnja. Rodney didn't come to the bench, instead, walking twenty or so yards down the touchline and sitting down. We lost 2-1.

It was a tremendous disappointment.

This time, we had enough to win. We should have won. But in order to have done so, we needed Rodney Marsh, the Rodney who was still our best player, not the Rodney of this day, the one I had grown all too familiar with in his last weeks at Queens Park Rangers. If anything, I was more frustrated than pleased when he went on that dribble, because it seemed to come so effortless to him. Where was that before? It seemed to me as if he were proving a point. If he really wanted to, he could have turned that game for us. And that was enough to really make my mind up to bring him off. In my opinion, his attitude wasn't right. Was he trying to pay the owner or the board back for refusing to give him his new deal? On the field he was one of the most instinctive players but off it, Rodney was cold and calculated. It seemed as if every decision was meticulously planned to maximize the attention he would receive. He would tell the younger players, "If you want to be noticed, be different."

Try as I might, Rodney had managed to overshadow another season of achievement for the Rowdies and make it about himself. On the night of his testimonial game, that was officially all about Rodney, he didn't disappoint—scoring two goals and showing the kind of form in entertaining the supporters that we desperately needed the previous week.

I received a letter from one member of the upper echelon whose name I won't mention; suffice to say, they expressed their pleasure that we were able to part ways with Marsh without uproar amongst the supporters. It was his decision, after all.

I haven't spoken to him since. The Tampa Bay Rowdies had a reunion dinner in August 2015 where we were both invited. It would have been interesting to meet up with him after all these years but he did not attend.

fourteen

Changes

IT WAS A time for change at Tampa Bay Rowdies with the loss of our talisman and the need for progression. It was also deemed necessary for some change by the powers that be within the structure of the game. The MISL (Major Indoor Soccer League) was growing in popularity and, not wanting to miss out, the NASL created their own indoor league with the teams made from a roster of the various club's (or franchise's) conventional outdoor squads. It was seen as a good way to keep the profile of the clubs up during the off-season and also a novel way of keeping the players active.

We weren't to know how quickly things would disintegrate because as the 1980 season approached, many in the NASL had the same optimism as we had at the Rowdies. The game had come on in leaps and bounds, the exposure was as great as it ever had been and now promising young stars were coming into the league early in their career with the prospect of playing with and against true legends of the game. Hugo Sanchez and Julio Cesar Romero were two such names. Sanchez, of course became a star at Real Madrid. Yes, many of the players were veterans, but their experience and abilities alongside these younger, developing players brought about a very high standard of play that in many cities attracted excellent crowds. The Cosmos would regularly get between forty and seventy thousand spectators a game.

It was a peak moment which should have been built upon but, instead, was a moment most identify as the commencement of the demise. But more on that later.

We didn't have the benefit of hindsight and so, entering the new decade, we embraced the changes and hoped they would be successful. We were the winners of the inaugural indoor season. However, we would never reach the collective heights that we did in 1979. We won the American Conference again for the third consecutive year but could only make the semifinals, missing out on the Soccer Bowl.

Tampa Bay Rowdies were in a decline that mirrored that of the NASL in general; clubs were folding left, right and center as years of overinvestment trying to compete with the likes of ourselves and the Cosmos caught up to various franchises.

The Washington Diplomats signed Johan Cruyff and a number of Dutch international players but engaging in that expense made them more observant of the overall finances. Their owner, Sonny Werblin, reasoned that when the Diplomats went to other cities, they would generally attract larger than usual attendances for the host team. So he arranged a meeting with owners of other clubs and proposed that the league should cut the number of teams and partake in revenue sharing. He felt there had been an expansion that occurred too swiftly. Too many new franchises were owned by non-soccer people who didn't understand about the losses and, inevitably, they couldn't sustain them.

I could agree with Sonny's long-term vision as it became increasingly clear that the existing model was not suitable for the long-term running of a league, but George Strawbridge was a little upset because he had many good friends who were owners of some of these so-called lesser franchises. Of course, part of the problem with just deciding to move a franchise from one state to another meant that establishing a consistent relationship with the local community was impossible. In recent years in England, that was seen when Wimbledon became the Milton Keynes Dons. But in the early 1980s, with the threat of collapse, this was happening everywhere in the NASL and the instances are too plentiful to mention. So, with no long-term vision, it was pointless trying to develop young players; an initiative was launched when the Diplomats folded (Werblin's proposal was dismissed, and he subsequently closed his franchise) to have "Team America" based in Washington. All of the teams in the NASL had to give up their promising young American players. Unfortunately this plan did not succeed.

It all came to a head in 1985 when only the Minnesota Strikers and Toronto Blizzard put up their bonds to play another year and so the NASL suspended the competition. There were plans to resurrect it but they never materialized.

Anyway, I digress. It seemed as if, in the near future in 1980, indoor soccer might prove to be just as popular. It was fast, packed with goals and grabbed the attention of the soccer supporter. In Europe we can appreciate that a 0-0 draw can be packed with its own excitement based on a wide degree of variables pertaining to the circumstances of the game. But it wasn't initially seen like that in North America and when these games of soccer suddenly seemed high scoring, the importance of them evolved from a worthwhile past-time between the longer than usual off-season to a genuine competition with a real desire to win.

Our desire was probably stronger than the other side's due to our disappointment from the Soccer Bowl defeats and we had some good skillful players who were capable of handling the difference. They handled it better than I did, that's for sure. For the first year coaching indoors, I didn't have a clue what I was doing. The tactics that were employed, the importance of substitutions and the timing of them. It wasn't alien to me, because at Queens Park Rangers and Millwall I'd enjoyed success at the London Football Clubs indoor championship played at Wembley arena each year and we always played five-a-side in training. Indoor obviously was different because of the boards and playing the game so competitively and it seriously called for an increased awareness of what methods brought success.

A change had been as good as a break when I went to Tampa in the first place but it wasn't enough throughout the year, going between the outdoor and the indoor game. We went from having an offseason that was too long to having none at all.

I grew physically and mentally tired. It affected my decision making. I let players go that I shouldn't have and wasn't as wise in my recruitment. That led to a disjointed dressing room with the wrong mix of characters. Out captain, a Dutch player, Jan van der Veen, was very demanding and at times very harsh when our younger players made mistakes. Van Der Veen was a very strong personality, able to exert his influence over matters on or off the field. As is probably evident by now, my method of management does not include screaming and shouting and I do not necessarily subscribe to the theory that fear is always a useful motivator for young players.

In 1981 I let Steve Wegerle go to the Cosmos to join Eddie Firmani and I cannot explain that decision because it was a mistake; the fans were keen to remind me with their banners at games.

June was equally quick to point out to me that I was looking as fatigued as I felt. Sometimes it needs somebody close to you to make you realize the truth about yourself and she was the person who did that. I faced up to it and knew that if I was so beset with this fatigue that I wasn't doing myself justice; I also wasn't doing the team justice, and so I felt it was the right decision to hand in my resignation. George must have felt the same because he asked me how I would feel about stepping down.

It was an amicable parting and I was pleased that George spoke well of me.

The truth was that I wasn't helping myself. I had taken on extra responsibilities, partnering in a recreational indoor soccer franchise and also a soccer travel agency. Perhaps, at the time, I was feeling more enthusiastic about those ventures, but with hindsight I can say with more certainty it was simply the fatigue. That much is probably proven by the fact that after leaving Tampa, I had a period of time away from the professional game altogether.

People speak about the NASL as if it were a failure.

It wasn't. it was a great success, without a doubt.

Yes, it folded. Yes, its demise, to a certain extent, was self-inflicted.

But the league brought about something that had never occurred until that point; organized youth soccer in the United States. It had been difficult, and near on impossible, to correlate this structure with the NASL with its transience, but a generation of young players were introduced to the game. The Indoor Leagues kept things going but the NASL was the beginning and it meant that when the Major Soccer League was established, there was already a nation of fledgling soccer players waiting for their big opportunities.

After all, what the NASL did do was provide spectators with the finest soccer ever seen in North America. It brought many top class players and coaches to the United States, who stayed on after the league folded and assisted in the development of the game to the level it has achieved today. Just look at the illustrious list of names—Pelé, George Best, Franz Beckenbauer, Carlos Alberto, Johan Neeskens, Bobby Moore, Rodney Marsh, Brian Kidd, Alan Ball, Gordon Banks, Dennis Viollett. And not forgetting Gordon Hill, Peter Beardsley, Hugo Sanchez, Steve Hunt, Roberto Cabanas and Julio Romero who were all there at the start of their careers.

Not every team had players of that caliber in their ranks of course but it stood to reason that in order to compete and not be embarrassed, some expense would have to be incurred. Additionally, there were costs of hiring stadiums and travel across the continent.

Some franchises weren't even strong enough to sustain that initial hit, which to me is the perfect example of people not knowing what they were getting themselves into. It wasn't the easy ride people were expecting. Disturbingly, some seemed to think of it as a cash cow. At that time, I became aware of financial irregularities at some clubs and I can bet that was just the tip of the iceberg. Illegal payments were made to agents and also to members of club's staff.

The Calgary Boomers went under after just one year with reported losses of $6 million. The general story was that $3 million of that was on general running expenses and $3 million was on player salaries and acquisitions. The initial plan was supposedly to spread that budget over three years but it was revised with the idea that if they invested it all at once, they'd have a better team and a possible championship. Of course it didn't work out like that and after twelve months, the franchise folded.

A meeting was held to discuss the futures of the contracted players and it was decided that they would be made available in a draft-style auction to all of the other clubs. Each player would be given a valuation which was disclosed; furthermore, all of the contract information of these players was also made open knowledge to all the NASL teams. The team with the worst record in the NASL got the first draft pick. If a player wasn't selected in the first draft, his "transfer fee" (which was going to the Boomers to help their debts) was halved in the second draft and again in each future round of the draft. It meant that some clubs obviously timed their bids tactically.

Five minutes before we were due to start this draft, the league Commissioner, Phil Woosnam, informed us that every player had a second contract.

Details of this second contract were private. This was against league rules. It was reported that all of the fees from this second contract were being paid to an agent in Switzerland. Where it went afterwards, nobody could tell. Did it remain with the agent? Did it go back to the player? Did it go back to the club?

The draft stopped completely. No team was prepared to make speculative bids on the unknown, and no team was prepared to enter into possibly illegal negotiations. The league ruled that all of the players were free agents and that the second contracts were null and void. The Calgary owner, Nelson Skalbania, lost everything. He had made mistakes by over-speculating but had done so innocently. Or, perhaps more to the point, naively.

Agents then took these players and offered them to the clubs. Say, for example, they offered a player for an acquisition fee of $30,000, the agent would then say discreetly to the general manager or head coach, "But we'll give you $5,000 of it."

There was another team where the general manager and coach were signing players but would only acquire them if the player agreed to return a percentage of the fee. To them it was as crooked as could be.

I was visited at my home in Tampa by an English agent in July 1980. He was very complimentary about it, and I said, "Well, if you think this is nice, you should see the show house—it's my wife's dream home!" He was even more impressed—it was 4000 square feet, the problems was that the only lot that I had found for it would cost $72,000. The agent went home and contacted me in September, telling me he had two players for me to see, one in Germany and one in Yugoslavia. I flew over to scout the players and although the one in German didn't interest me, the Yugoslavian did. I enquired about his price with the agent.

"He's $400,000, and there's $72,000 in it for you in cash. Payable anywhere in the world," I was told.

I could have shook hands on that deal and nobody would have batted an eyelid. Acquisition fees were not common in American sports. This was an international player. The agent said that he did these deals in England all of the time. The inference was that if I accepted this, I could expect this all of the time. If I had accepted that deal I would not only have been cheating but also stealing money from George Strawbridge. How could I do that to a man who had shown me such wonderful generosity? Here was a man who had demonstrated eagerness to have me coach his team and, every Christmas, would give me plane tickets to take my family back to London. He was a class man.

"I'll give you $300,000, but forget me," I said to the agent.

I never heard another word.

The Calgary story is open for anyone to see, though no one can say with any sort of certainty where the money eventually went. I wasn't in a position to blow the whistle on it because I would have required hard evidence to open that particular can of worms. Now, so much time has passed that it will serve no purpose to name names. Barely a week went by without an agent knocking on your door offering you players, trying to exploit this lack of knowledge in the owners.

Combine those losses, which were substantial, to the run-of-the-mill costs which were already hurting owners who were quickly realizing that, by and large, owning a football club wasn't a profitable venture at that time.

Lack of knowledge and awareness of these things that could be so ruthlessly exploited without any regulation led to the rapid dissolution and I am left in no doubt that the events at Calgary were probably happening elsewhere. It crippled the NASL at a time when it quite literally couldn't afford it; it was vulnerable enough as it was in the early 1980's.

Those were the lessons that would have to be learned if the NASL would return from its hiatus or if a major professional league in the United States would ever be properly established again.

From an initiative point of view, I feel it bears repeating that the NASL was a great success, and that its history plays a fundamentally crucial role in the current status of the United States club game.

fifteen

No Enjoyment of Profession

IT TOOK ME a little while to regain my enthusiasm for soccer. I had enjoyed a resurgence in Tampa but my tiredness was also accompanied by a certain sense of disillusion with the financial side of the game and witnessing how it was being exploited.

The fatigue was an issue that I have to take responsibility for. Although the promotional side was handled by the marketing staff, I enjoyed getting involved where possible and doing as much as I could. And, with the indoor season, I felt a duty of responsibility as coach to continue to work. It was too much. There is an irony there, as having fewer official responsibilities was part of the attraction of returning to the United States. The lines were blurred because I had enjoyed those first two years so much. I had deliberately stayed out of the promotional activities, other than enjoying them as much as any spectator would, but, as a natural workaholic, I wanted to dedicate as much of my time as I could in order to make the team a success.

In the UK I'd been heralded as a pioneer and I did like that. I liked that I was seen as someone not afraid to introduce new things, that I was the first to do something new. It didn't always work. I had observed how it was a rule that the press were allowed access to the dressing room in American sports and at Queens Park Rangers I tried to implement that procedure. It was awkward to put into practice in soccer in the UK, and so we canned that idea after just two games. They didn't embrace it, or perhaps I didn't provide enough assistance to articulate how it would work best. But as a coach, an employee of the club, I saw my commitment to be one which would assist the on pitch and off pitch success of it. With the Rowdies, that extended to building a successful indoor and outdoor team and being the coach of both of those sides. The North American game still had some way to go to match European standards (not least of which were some of the rule changes it resisted to conform) but I was able to fully concentrate on getting my team to play the style of football I enjoyed. That much had never changed.

Mind you, perhaps it was made a little easier by the lack of knowledge in "pundits" at that time. I never received criticism for any defeats or the style of play on my team. I remember once being interviewed on television and there were three presenters, one never asked a single question, as he simply wasn't educated enough in the game to think of something worthwhile to contribute. That's not being mean, or rotten, the United States was trying novel things with television but they simply didn't have the knowledge of the game at the time to truly capitalize on the great ideas they did have.

Anyway, the point of all of this was that the extracurricular activities had worn me down. I wasn't really looking for another coaching position but was contacted regarding an opportunity that had arisen at Queens Park Rangers. My old player Terry Venables had been manager at Queens Park Rangers and had done so well that he had been appointed the manager at Barcelona.

I was still living in Tampa but was considering moving back to England anyway. Word got to Jim Gregory, who was still the chairman, and he invited me over. I stayed at his house for a week, and we talked about possibilities going forward. I insisted I wanted nothing to do with the management of the team. I was more interested in the promotional side of it. I felt I had a lot to offer on the marketing side and Jim was immediately all for it. He agreed straight away and on the second night I was there he called my wife to tell her he was looking forward to having me back.

At the end of my stay he drove me to Heathrow airport and asked how quickly I could return. We drove through Epsom and he was pointing out places I could live.

"Who should we appoint as coach?" he also asked.

I recommended David Pleat. Jim interviewed him, but David turned him down.

I arrived back in Florida and commenced arrangements to sell our house and move back to London. I received a phone call from Jim's son on my second day back.

"Dad's going on holiday," I was told. "And the job's no longer available."

Familiar?

I don't know what happened. Maybe some people thought I was after the manager's role; maybe others thought I wanted to take their job on the marketing staff.

I was also contacted by Jack Petchey, a director at West Ham United, inviting me to come and join their marketing staff, but it appeared that he couldn't persuade the board. I would have loved for that to have happened. West Ham was my boyhood club, after all.

At that point in my life, 52 years old, I felt that I had done all I wanted to with regards o coaching in soccer. I had observed that it was around 55 years of age when many managers would start to suffer from health problems with the stresses the game brought.

That perception correlated with my mindset; I'd simply been away from the English game too long to be considered for top level jobs even if I had the enthusiasm. If I was out of sight and out of mind for English clubs, then, similarly, my knowledge of the game in my homeland—which players I ought to scout, the best teams—was not as great as it could have been.

⚽ ⚽ ⚽

I had no way of knowing at the time that when I brought a little-known forward from Brazil by the name of Tatu to the United States, how synonymous we would become.

The Tampa Bay Rowdies did a deal with Sao Paulo of Brazil where we would get three players on loan, and we would send them six young players who would train with them to gain experience, as well as send down some of our marketing team to give them promotional advice.

I went down to Sao Paulo for twelve days and selected the three best players from their first team, all internationals. I was watching a small-sided game on a basketball court with the small goals and there was this youngster who was absolutely brilliant.

"Who's that?" I asked the coach.

"That's Tatu, he's 18 . . . not quite ready for the first team."

I told him I'd love to have him for our indoor team and they arranged for that to take place. When it came around to May in 1981, and time for the selected stars to join us in time for the new outdoor season, Sao Paulo reneged on their deal.

In desperation to salvage something from the deal, I asked if we could have Tatu on an extra year's loan, with an option to buy him for a $30,000 transfer fee. He had built up an incredible reputation in his short time indoors for us but was still untested in the outdoors game and I preferred a year's loan to assess his outdoor soccer ability before a possible purchase. The start to a long termed association between us.

Shortly after that missed opportunity with West Ham I received a phone call from Bill Nuttall who had been a coach at Fort Lauderdale Strikers. He had applied for the vacant head coach position at the Dallas Sidekicks, an indoor soccer team. He was unsuccessful but was hired as the player personnel director. The Sidekicks really wanted a young ex-player, Kyle Rote, Jr. to be their head coach, but he was taking too long in making a decision. So they called me, but I politely declined the opportunity. Two days later, Bill and the general manager of the Sidekicks turned up on my doorstep in Tampa.

"All we ask is that you hear us out and come and meet the club owner," they asked.

I talked it over with June, who had also been invited, and we agreed to go and meet the owner, Don Carter. Mr. Carter owned the Dallas Mavericks and had purchased the New Jersey Rockets soccer franchise, relocating them to Texas.

Mr. Carter was a good old boy from Texas. I'd heard some stories about him, how he would suddenly stop in mid-conversation and sometimes insult you. I thought it a strange thing to mention but sure enough, in our meeting, he suddenly stopped speaking. I just sat, waiting for him to talk.

"Don't you think you're too old?" he suddenly said.

"No, I think I have the ability to coach," I replied. It wasn't exactly an insult but it was a curious thing for him to say.

The meeting went on and reached its natural conclusion.

"Mr. Carter," I said, as I stood to leave. "I've been very fortunate to have had longevity in most of the jobs that I've had. I've had very few interviews. But I'll tell you this, it's certainly been the most interesting."

Afterwards, June and I arranged to go to the airport. Bill was to pick us up and drop us off there, so I called him.

"Bill, we're all ready to go."

"No, no, Mr. Carter wants you! You've got the job."

They wanted to move me from the hotel I was in to another more obscure one so we could surprise the players and the press. They asked me to stay on a couple more days so we could attend a press conference.

I was hired in August with the league due to start in October. Bill had assembled the team but it wasn't good enough; there were too many boys fresh out of college who hadn't played indoors. We played a few practice games and I could see we weren't good enough.

I approached Mr. Carter and confessed my concerns.

"We'll take our licks," he said, in his broad Texan accent. "If they come off the field and crawl up the corridor with blood on their knees then it's fine by me. But if they run up the corridor and go out dancing then get rid of 'em."

He expected people to work hard, as he had in his own life, but he was very supportive with it.

We lost the first ten games. We had 12 wins and 36 losses in that first year. The atmosphere was terrible, we were playing in front of just 1700 fans.

There are many differences between the indoor and outdoor game but some things ring true for both. Indeed, in almost any occupation, given time, an able employee will improve and do a good job. Time, that worst of enemies, and time, that best of friends. Things improved in my second year with 25 victories and 23 losses but we still weren't great. I never suffered from any apprehension. I never thought that I'd made the wrong choice. I always maintained that it didn't always matter if there was a problem, so long as I could identify it; in identifying it, I would be able to solve it.

That confidence came with my experience, and I was still as confident coaching indoors as I had been outdoors, although I must confess it took a while to adapt. In that first year I learned so much from the way other teams played against us, and also, I watched a lot of ice hockey to see if there was anything we could adapt, particularly on power plays. The first year was a nightmare.

I recruited a number of players I had worked with at Tampa Bay—Wes McLeod, Perry van der Beck, Pedro DeBrito, Mark Karpun and Tatu. They improved us but they, like I, were on a learning curve. There were many subtle tricks applied by teams, using whatever advantages they could find. Some teams would take calculated risks on rebounds, taking advantage of the rolling substitute to take off a defender and put on an attacker to exploit a counterattack. We were punished by our naivety on that front a few times in the first year. Or, players using the rebound off the boards to either pass the ball to a teammate or outfox a defender.

Consequently, hopes of relying on a good defense go out of the window. The indoor game is heavily based on offense. You have to have organization, of course, but you accept that you will concede a high number of goals in games. The most important thing is concentration and this goes for every player in the team. Never leave your teammates outnumbered or vulnerable.

Substitutions, and the timing of them, was crucial too, as was the stamina and conditioning of the players. You cannot expect a player to play for the entire game. In some instances you have to be prepared to go on the field and then very quickly come off again if you are presented with a situation to gain a man up situation. The players were learning as much as I was.

Bill Nuttell had hastily put that squad together so it was inevitable that even with my changes and a year's worth of experience, some wouldn't be good enough to bring us success in the long term. Mr. Carter had seen enough in terms of progress to at least justify giving me time.

Even in those defeats, there were signs of optimism. Tatu was already showing what a capable player I knew him to be in the indoor game. We might lose 10-3 but he'd be the one scoring our goals. He also had a gimmick where he would toss his jersey into the crowd after every goal that he scored and then come and get a new one to play on with. So, if we were playing away from Dallas and were heavily beaten, it would still be our goal to be shown on the television because of Tatu throwing his jersey. He gained a reputation for that although his football did the talking. Behind Steve Zungul, the star player at San Diego, Tatu was far and away the second best player in the major indoor soccer league. He was brilliant and it was a delight to have him.

We implemented a clearly understood rotational system within our squad of fifteen players. The game moves at such speed that a coach cannot make substitutions. He doesn't have the time. You have to trust the players to know when it's the optimum time to substitute. As coach, your main concern is whether a player is staying on for too long, rather than constantly arranging the changes. You are more concerned about the shape of the side, whether to commit an extra player in offense or defense depending on the score. It's much more constant than the outdoor game. To all intents and purposes it's a different game altogether.

Of course, having a player like Tatu on our side meant that our game plan was always to make the most of his ability. We'd try and get the ball played up to him as he moved from the center to a wing position. He was so good at receiving the ball and moving with it that the opposition would often put an extra man on him. That meant we were left with one spare, so we would plan for a player to arrive in support and exploit the space that way. Of course, Tatu was so good he often didn't need help. He was adept at spinning and shooting towards the far post. As they always do, the success of your tactics relies on the ability of your players, and Tatu's skill played such an important part in the team's success.

I would often tell friends who came to see our games not to expect anything like the outdoor game. The differences were vast. In training there was an intense concentration on drills. Organization, using rebounds, and free kicks. Over and over again. Repetition was very important. To consider it from this point of view, one can appreciate it is closer to the more popular American sports than it is to soccer, which finds its own popularity in the creative and unpredictable. That's not to say that the unpredictable can't be just as impressive indoors.

The first two years hadn't brought much success on the field but we were starting to move in the right direction. I was given the honor of being named head coach of the year in my second season for the improvement we had made but I was just happy to be enjoying my work again. As someone who is enthusiastic about learning, I embraced these changes and was excited by them. Gradually, our supporters grew excited too, though I do think that they were very patient with us.

Certainly, when success did come, it was ahead of schedule. We played three teams in the playoffs, in the regular season, we had played six times against each of those teams and our record against them all was one win and five losses. To say we were underdogs, then, was something of an understatement. The playoffs were best of five and in the first two rounds and then best of seven in the final. This format helped take the pressure off of us. A one game playoff would have been difficult. We defeated Baltimore Blast three games to two in the Division semifinal and then in the Divisional Final defeated Cleveland Force by four games to one to qualify for the Championship Series against Tacoma Stars.

It was going to take a miracle to defeat them as they seemed so much stronger than us. But, just as at Tampa Bay Rowdies, it was a miracle we were in the Championship Series at all. Partly because of the quality of the teams we faced and our previous record against them but also because Mr. Carter had to sell the franchise in June 1986 and only an intervention from a group of new owners saved the Sidekicks, which showed how much we had grown to mean to our local supporters.

Sadly the first two games of the Championship Series in Tacoma went to form. We were hammered 10-4 and then 7-4 by Tacoma. Back in Dallas, with our home support, we were able to tie the Series with two narrow wins, 5-3 and 6-3. In the fifth game in Tacoma, they won 5-3, fortunately we equaled the series in the sixth game back in Dallas with a nervy 4-3 victory. In that last game, they were leading 3-2 but we scored a late equalizer to tie the game. It was an incredible game and went into double overtime. Mark Karpun scored after more than twenty minutes to send the series into a decider.

We traveled back to Tacoma with both teams knowing that home advantage had proved crucial each time. In the final seventh game with two minutes and thirty-three seconds left on the clock, we were losing 3-1. I decided that there was nothing left to lose and we'd pull the goalkeeper to play with an extra outfielder, but we couldn't even get the ball back to the "keeper" in order to take a time out! When we finally did, Krys Sobieski our excellent goal keeper, instead of putting his foot on the ball, the procedure to take a timeout, he picked up the ball so for that moment we lost being able to call for a time out! Fortunately a few seconds later we were able to take a time out and make the change. Against all odds we scored; Tacoma attempted to keep possession but in their haste, kicked the ball out and into their own bench, meaning that we got a free kick. From that mistake we capitalized, scoring in the final seconds to tie the game.

We had saved the game but we couldn't afford to go without the goalkeeper throughout overtime. Tacoma had four players who had each scored more than forty goals in the season, led by Zungul, the greatest of them all.

I looked up and saw that there were hundreds of balloons ready to be released in victory celebration for our hosts. There had been a public address for the Tacoma owners to come down for the trophy presentation, in front of a sellout crowd of 21,728. It was, and remains, a record crowd for an indoor game.

When Mark Karpun struck in a tense overtime period to win the game for us, there was a moment where it all felt so surreal.

We were champions.

A video was released to commemorate that year and it was given the title "Never Say Die," which, given the numerous events that had unfolded, seemed very apt indeed.

"If you live to be a hundred years old, you'll never live through another experience such as this one," I told our players and supporters at our victory parade.

It was incredible. The achievement was up there with my finest in football but it represented a truly communal effort from those who had been in the team from the start. With our collective limited knowledge of the game, to go from 12 wins and 36 losses to 25 wins and 23 losses then to 28 wins and 24 losses and only narrowly making the playoffs to our ultimate triumph in the space of three years marked a progression that I don't think anybody had a right to expect.

More than five thousand supporters welcomed us at the Dallas Airport. We couldn't believe the reception. As we flew over the airport we had noticed, painted on the runway, "GO SIDEKICKS."

sixteen

Cometh the Hour

We were unable to repeat our heroics over the next couple of years but I think that represented the significance of our achievement in the first place. When the Sidekicks came under another new ownership in 1989, I was asked if I would concentrate more on the promotional aspect and helping to build the profile of the team locally. Billy Phillips, who had been our goalkeeper in our Championship team, and later, my assistant coach, became the head coach.

But it was the instability in our ownership which presented the biggest headache. After Mr. Carter, Stan Finney took over. Then David Paschal, then Phil Cobb. Then Mr. Carter came back and saved us in 1991. Phil Cobb had decided he couldn't afford to run the franchise any longer. Without us, the league would have folded, because the other six teams had told the commissioner that if there were only six teams in the league, they would not participate.

The *USA Today* newspaper ran a story that the Dallas Sidekicks would fold and so would the league because we couldn't attract new ownership. Mr. Carter was in South Carolina on business. He went down to breakfast and saw the newspaper, called his secretary and insisted that she get hold of me.

Mr. Carter called me at 9 am.

"What's this I read in the paper?"

"Well unfortunately it's true," I admitted. "I do have one gentleman prepared to put up 50% but I can't get the other fifty percent."

"What would I get for my fifty percent?"

"You've been there before, Mr. Carter, it will be the same," I replied.

"I've got to fly from here to New York and from there to St. Louis. But tell the commissioner I'll be calling back when I land," he informed me.

At 2 pm Mr. Carter called me and said he'd spoken to the commissioner. "We're okay. We're in business. I'll see you when I get back."

It was a tremendous relief after years of insecurity. One year, the staff did not receive any wages in the summer because there was technically no club. I went on local television pleading for investors. So, I was very relieved when Mr. Carter came back, although he must have had some cross words to face from his wife. He had faced a lot of criticism when he let go of the club the first time around.

With Mr. Carter back as the owner, I returned as head coach once again, with Billy as my assistant. That was all that *was* familiar. The league had struggled internally with disputes amongst rival owners and so a breakaway league was established named the Continental Indoor Soccer League. We won the CISL in its inaugural season; after going 3 and 3 in our first six games, we proceeded to win twenty of our remaining twenty-two. That's me all over, isn't it—a slow start and a strong finish! We then defeated Monterrey in the playoffs and San Diego in the Championship Series. A fine year that was capped off nicely when I was voted coach of the year again.

I was pleased with my accomplishment but I feel that the stability provided by Mr. Carter's return was more important.

In history, there have been many great people who have come forth in moments of need.

Although you cannot compare the needs of a sport to those of major world concerns many key men have taken leadership roles when their sport was in need.

Those examples can be of significant importance to the team they are affiliated with, such as with Mr. Carter and the Dallas Sidekicks, or significant to the sport itself.

In the case of the sport of football/soccer, men such as Sir Alex Ferguson and Sir Matt Busby, both building a magnificent club, Manchester United both on and off the field from 1946 to 2013; Gustav Sebes, who along with outstanding players Ferenc Puskas and Nandor Hidegkuti developed Hungarian soccer to one of the highest levels of world soccer. They went undefeated at home for seventeen years and had a record of only one defeat in 48 games during the 1950s. And Rinus Michels, who built the Dutch club Ajax and the Holland National team into powerhouses in the 1960s with a total soccer style much admired throughout world soccer.

All came to the forefront of the sport of football/soccer to take the sport to a new level and worldwide acclaim.

Today, world football/soccer is the number one sport in terms of participation, financial wealth and acclaim. Every four years the FIFA World Cup finals attract a TV audience of over 2.5 billion viewers.

Club teams such as Real Madrid of Spain and Manchester United are two of the richest sports franchises (or clubs, or teams, whichever definition you prefer) in the world. All thanks to men in control of those clubs and organizations who have taken their team and Federations to such a high level of performance and worldwide recognition.

Who are the men in recent years that should receive those same accolades for achieving similar success?

In my opinion one man has already achieved that status in the USA and another will join him in the upcoming years.

The United States of America is a newly recognized member of the World soccer community. Yes, the game dates back to 1837 with the game being played at Harvard University and the USA 1-0 victory over mighty England in the World Cup finals played in Brazil in 1950.

That will remain in soccer folklore forever, but in the early 1900s, US soccer was an amateur sport played by ex-patriots in a number of the old large American cities such as Chicago, St. Louis, New York and Philadelphia. Only now, in recent years, is American soccer making its mark on the world soccer stage.

The major turning point was the selection of the United States to host the 1994 World Cup Finals. Little did FIFA, the governing body of world soccer, know at that time that the tournament played in twelve US cities across the country would become one of the finest organized World Cup Finals with 3.6 million fans attending the 52 games. With $50 million dollars profit, it was the most financially successful World Cup Finals of all time.

Let us go back in time. With the recent controversy that has surrounded the World Cups that have been awarded to Russia and Qatar, I feel it may be helpful to explain as best as I can the path of events which led to the USA getting the tournament in 1994.

In 1980 the United States was selected to hold the 1984 summer Olympics games. Included in the many sports to be organized was the sport of soccer, but with amateur players. There were no professional paid players whatsoever. With the increase of professional soccer around the world, the Olympic committee decided that the competition and nations could include professional players for the first time. However, their rules stated that no players could have played in more than five international games prior to their selection. Olympic soccer would be the highest level of soccer ever seen at the four venue cities across the United States.

Peter Ueberroth, the US Olympic Sports Chairman/President selected a close friend to take control of the organization of the Olympic soccer finals to be played in four US cities. It was a decision that proved to be one of the many excellent decisions he made in his tenure.

The man selected was Alan Rothenberg, an attorney with a Los Angeles law firm, and a former part-owner of the North American Soccer League team the Los Angeles Aztecs. He put together a first class group of people to take the responsibility of organizing the tournament. With attention to detail, excellent media, PR and game promotion the tournament was a huge success, multiple sellouts of over 100,000 fans at the Pasadena Rose Bowl with 1,425,181 fans attending the 32 games played, an average game attendance of 44,537.

This success did not go unnoticed at FIFA headquarters in Zurich and a movement behind the scenes commenced to put Alan Rothenberg's name forward as a candidate for the position of President of the United States Soccer Federation.

With the 1994 World Cup finals being allocated to the United States the United States Soccer Federation Annual General Meeting in 1990 in Orlando took on a new importance. The incumbent president Werner Fricker, with strong support of the established soccer communities in the Midwest and eastern regions behind him, was a strong favorite to be reelected.

The elected President would be the key man in the organization and control of the 1994 USA World Cup finals. He would be recommending to the FIFA organizing committee, the twelve cities to be the venues selected. He would be responsible for the appointment of leaders and staff at each venue, an increase in USSF headquarters staff, selection of official hotels in each of the selected cities, contracts for companies involved in improving stadium facilities to FIFA stated standards, selection of companies to produce official merchandise, stadium concessions contracts, the legal documentation of almost every aspect of staging the game across the USA. There were so many major concerns to think about in order to organize a successful World Cup finals tournament.

The USSF was about to become a very important and powerful organization with the president of the USSF being the man to oversee all the necessary new appointments and all the contracts issued to so many companies that would be involved.

With the FIFA support for Alan Rothenberg, in view of his success in the organization of the 1984 Olympic games' soccer tournament, they were attempting to set the stage for the USSF Annual General Meeting (AGM) president election. At the same time, there was a rumor that Werner Fricker was not the most liked at FIFA meetings during the 1990 World Cup finals in Italy. That rumor may have been a deliberate ploy by certain FIFA officials to assist in getting their choice, Alan Rothenberg, elected. A further rumor spread at the USSF Annual General Meeting on the day before the elections that if Werner Fricker was reelected as president, FIFA may take the World Cup finals away from the United States.

With only four years before the USA finals and so much already in place I could not believe that could happen but with the election vote to take place the very next day, such a rumor could sway some of the delegates representing the fifty state soccer associates in attendance. It was a staggering insight into how political some aspects had become.

We now know that with the total support of the Major Indoor Soccer League, the only professional soccer league with membership of the USSF at that time, plus support of a key number of states associations such as Florida, North Texas and South California, Alan Rothenberg was elected President of the USSF in 1990.

Whether Werner Fricker could have brought about the same success of the 1994 USA World Cup finals as Alan Rothenberg, will of course never be known, but in my opinion Alan Rothenberg brought about a very high standard of business and sports professionalism to the USSF, something that had never been in place before.

As part of the initial FIFA agreement to give the 1994 World Cup finals to the United States, the USSF had to guarantee that a major professional soccer league would be in place across the USA by the year 1995/96. This was achieved and Major Indoor Soccer League celebrated its 21st year in 2016.

Cometh the hour, cometh the man.

As someone who now had a strong history in the Dallas soccer community and was fairly well known throughout the soccer world, when the United States won the right to stage the 1994 World Cup Finals, I was entrusted with some responsibilities with regards to local promotion. I considered it an honor, as I did when I was give a place on the CONCACAF coaching committee although my position was more ceremonial and my actual involvement was quite minimal.

In Dallas, I was in charge of a World Cup speakers' bureau and involved with British television in getting all their TV and radio staff into the best hotels. It had been suggested that I should stand for the USSF presidential election myself but that would have been totally wrong. I thought Alan Rothenburg was the right man and I said as much in our meetings where I was the representative for the Dallas Sidekicks. I had already decided to vote for him before I heard the Fricker rumors, but, in our MISL meeting, we were all strongly advised by the league commissioner Earl Foreman to vote for Fricker.

"Why?" I asked.

"Because he's a good man and I think he will do a good job . . . and, additionally, I've arranged a deal with him where the US national team will play two outdoor games against an MISL team with all the proceeds going to the league."

It wasn't a convincing enough argument. And I was concerned that any vote for Fricker could mean "goodbye World Cup" for the United States.

It would have been a disaster and the argument to support Fricker simply wasn't strong enough.

Thankfully the other six teams' representatives agreed with me and we all voted for Alan Rothenburg. Then, strangely enough, our commissioner immediately met with him and agreed to the same deal with him as he had with Fricker! Soccer politics! I also went to see the presidents of the Texas and Florida state local football authorities to lobby for votes for Alan.

The result of the vote shocked many people who thought that Fricker would gain the presidency. After the result, I was confronted by one of the USSF vice presidents who told me in no uncertain manner that she felt I had personally been involved with Fricker's failure to be reelected.

Alan was criticized because he was partner in the law firm that made money through contracts that had been agreed for the World Cup but that didn't concern me. He was the right man for the job as was proven by the tremendous success of the tournament.

I also had the opportunity to work on radio commentary with Jon Champion for the BBC at the World Cup and really enjoyed myself. To be as involved as I was made me feel really proud, to simply say the tournament was a big success doesn't reveal the scale of the accomplishment. This was a "non soccer country," remember? And Dallas' own role in it all, as the base for world communications, made me just as proud of my city as I was of the country. As usual, the United States didn't fail when it came to putting on a show.

seventeen

Commissioner Gordon Jago

I HAD INTENDED to retire from coaching in my mid 50s but I continued with the Sidekicks until well into my 60s. Admittedly, the pressures of the game were not anywhere near as great as they had been in the outdoor game but I had invested my time so heavily into the Sidekicks, particularly in the early 90s, that before I knew it I'd spent longer there than I had with any outdoor soccer team.

I had been with the Dallas Sidekicks, after all, since the franchise was created in 1984.

The Continental Indoor Soccer League ceased in 1997 and the "Premier Soccer Alliance" (later renamed the World Indoor Soccer League) was formed in its place. Some of the owners of the other teams approached Mr. Carter and the new co-owner of the Sidekicks, Sonny Williams, and asked if they would consider allowing me to be the commissioner of the new league.

Tatu was finishing as a player and the homogenous and natural progression to being the coach was something I felt was necessary in order to keep the Sidekicks supporters connected to the team. It was also important to the owners that the next coach be such a recognizable figure.

It was the right time for me to step away from coaching, and, always having had a fondness for organization, I was enthusiastic about this new challenge. I was very proud to be elected by the fellow teams as it was a reflection of what I hoped was a just and fair attitude. They knew I wouldn't be "pro-Sidekicks" in the role. It was a very small office but we ran the league in terms of rules and scheduling. We ran the league on a shoestring but we knew what we were doing and I think it worked well.

I served three years in the role before the League merged with the six remaining franchises from the non-defunct National Professional Soccer League to form the Major Indoor Soccer League. I stepped aside to allow the commissioner from the NPSL continue his role.

Though I had operated without bias the Sidekicks remained an important part of my life and I was pleased to see that the owners and Tatu strived for the team's survival as much as I had. When they enjoyed success in 1998 and 2001 winning the World Indoor Soccer League (WISL) Championships, nobody was as pleased as I was. We were looked upon as the top franchise and, at that time, we also became the longest continuously running franchise in soccer of any sort in the United States.

Sadly, I recognized some familiar mistakes creeping in at a time when I was powerless to influence change. Nonsoccer people came into the game, the new commissioner of the MISL was a prime example. He enforced strange rules which alienated teams and, I felt that he did not have a great enough understanding of the game. When we did try to speak up, the reply was generally, "What do you know?" with the implication that we'd somehow been responsible, at least in part, for the dissolution of previous leagues.

We were sadly proven correct.

I wasn't involved with the club so I wasn't privy to the inner workings which led to the demise of the Sidekicks in 2004, nor would I care to speculate as to why it transpired. I can only comment as the observer I was at that point—then involved with the Dallas Cup—and say how tremendously sad it was to hear of the news. We had fought so often and so strongly to maintain the operations of the club and to see it close therefore did evoke a real sadness. The owner Mr. Williams, had, along with Mr. Carter, given the club more years than it might have had. Having worked with them both so closely and of course having been so involved in trying to attract new owners at various times, I could appreciate the financial difficulty involved.

As we have seen in England with the controversy surrounding the owner of Hull City wanting to change their name to the "Tigers," the will of the owner sometimes dictates shifting heritages. In the United States, we've seen it time and time again with franchises that were sold off and relocated and thus renamed. Sometimes, if the franchise wasn't successful, the owner would simply want to disassociate himself from it and create a new legacy. Then, in 2012, a few of us who had those long-standing connections with the Sidekicks were contacted by an investment group looking at reestablishing the franchise. I was asked if I would provide color commentary for the TV broadcasting and Tatu was approached to be coach again.

There is a disparity in the league. The Sidekicks have done well since returning but have struggled against the top teams; it's a case of qualifying for the playoffs, but as soon as they come up against a full-time professional team, they are defeated. The difference is notable. They are getting there and I think a large part of their progress and success will be in part because of the heritage they retained, or took on, when reestablishing the club. There are supporters now who were youngsters when I was coach; they bring their children. There are so many familiar faces and I enjoy seeing old friends as much as I enjoy watching the game.

eighteen

The MLS

THOUGH MY OCCUPATION and primary interests were invested in the Sidekicks in the late nineties, I was delighted to see the rebirth of the outdoor game with the formation of Major League Soccer. It has gone from strength to strength and, to my mind, has benefitted from people not making the same mistakes as were made with the NASL. If the MLS had failed on its rebirth there is no telling where soccer would be in the United States today.

That's not to say there isn't concern. I do feel that expansion has come too quickly and furthermore, that there isn't sufficient quality coming through at the standard which is required to populate MLS teams. The college system is not geared towards supporting expansions and further franchises; it's debatable whether it was sufficient as it was and that, to me, threatens to weaken the product. The object of the exercise is to develop youngsters in college to get them in a position where they are ready for the MLS in the same way that in American Football they are ready for the NFL. That to me will require a fundamental change in the approach to coaching within colleges.

If, in the short term, it is a losing battle to regulate soccer development in the same way as it is in Europe (and I accept that logistically, with the nature of soccer being the most popular sport and a working class sport with so many local teams, it cannot be expected that a country the size of the United States can immediately adopt this approach), then I feel it is of paramount importance that colleges employ top class soccer coaches. It's difficult enough with the competition to get the best athletes playing soccer. The top sports in North America are hand-ball games—basketball, football and baseball (coincidentally, this is undoubtedly why the US National team has always had a top class goalkeeper).

It's no surprise that parents will want their children to be developed by better coaches and developed for a career with greater prospects, so soccer is losing a great number of athletes for these reasons.

Now don't get me wrong. Youth soccer in the US has only really existed since 1972 and the generation of kids who grew up watching soccer as a popular sport were probably born in the 70s and 80s so it's fairly logical that the best US players at present are players born from that era.

It is in that generational development, which can only come with time, that we will see greater talent come through. Because now, players who have experienced top international soccer in recent years such as Landon Donovan, Tim Howard and Clint Dempsey, can use that experience to assist in the development of the soccer stars of tomorrow.

Gordon Jago enjoying a cup of tea with Manchester City manager Joe Mercer following the Queens Park Rangers versus Manchester City game in 1974.

Gordon at the London Sportsmen's Dinner at the Café Royale, London, alongside Alan Mullery, manager of Fulham FC and Derek Ibbotson, Great Britain Olympic runner.

The Football League Manager of the Month trophy is awarded to Gordon in March 1976. Helping him hold it is Barry Kitchener, Millwall FC captain.

The announcement lunch at which Gordon was introduced as Head Coach of the Tampa Bay Rowdies, alongside wife, June, and daughter, Kim.

(*Left*) Enjoying the Florida weather in March 1978, Gordon, daughter Kim and wife June.

(*Below*) Tampa Bay Rowdie fans celebrate at the Tampa Bay Stadium as the Rowdies defeat Ft. Lauderdale in the 1978 North American Soccer League (NASL) semifinals.

(*Left*) Gordon getting his message across during the 1978 season and with Dave Miller (*below left*)

nineteen

US Youth Soccer is in a Mess

If I Were Coaching a Youth Team, I Would Wish to Have Eleven Orphans in the Team

A STRONG VIEW and a strong desire brought about from attending so many youth soccer games. I have witnessed in recent years:

- Two fathers fighting at a U-14 boy's game.
- A watching father ejected from a U-16 boys game for bad language—ten minutes after the start of the game.
- A boy's mother berating the team coach for keeping her son on the bench.
- Parents shouting to their children to "knock her down," "Don't let them push you around," and "Don't let him beat you, take him down."
- The mother of a U-13 boy goalkeeper storming into the office of Dallas Cup Tournament Manager Randy Jones, demanding that the red card issued to her son for pulling down an opposing forward in the penalty area be rescinded. She stated that the college coaches at the tournament who were apparently scouting potential scholarship recruiters would now not see her son for he would be suspended from the next game. A 13-year-old! College coaches are not looking for recruits until 16 or 17 years of age.

But these incidents are just a few examples of the appalling behavior of some parents at youth sports games every week all over the USA and it occurs in all competitive sports in the United States, not just soccer.

The chants of "We are number one" whenever victory is achieved. The pressure put on their children to win instead of telling them to just enjoy their game and have fun. I am told that many young boys and girls dread the ride home in the family car following a game, such is the criticism by the parents if their youngster has lost the game or not performed to the standard that they wish.

The lack of discipline, the bad language, the terrible attitude of the parents to losing and the pressure they apply to their children, are all the wrong lessons that one should show and teach to their children. These are not only the wrong lessons in life but in so many cases their behavior turns their children away from the sport. It is not fun and enjoyment to participate if there is a fear of failure and criticism. These are young children who should be given the opportunity to experience all sports, to have fun, learn team spirit, be humble in victory and learn the disappointment of losing and receiving a "well done" if they have given of their best.

Parents have a responsibility in my opinion to educate their children in the correct behavior to others at all times, to conduct themselves properly in respecting other people.

Unfortunately at too many games of many sports, not only soccer, we see this terrible behavior of parents, setting disgraceful examples of how not to behave. I wonder if they ever see that maybe they were the problem if their child does grow up with a behavior or discipline concerns?

My advice to all parents at their children's games is to be supportive and encouraging. Cheer them on and a word of support if a mistake is made or a game is lost. Teach them to congratulate their opponents if they have been successful and as previously stated be humble in victory.

The lessons that you teach in those early days are important to your children as they go through life. Surely you wish to be proud of them as they grow into adults and remember it is your early lessons that can bring that about.

If we are able to assist the parents to act correctly then we also have to somehow bring about an improvement in the conduct of the team coaches involved in US youth soccer, as with parents at games we also see appalling conduct of coaches. I suppose, in that respect, you can understand how and why the parents behave in such a way if that is what they are being subjected to seeing as the "norm." They are witnessing their children being supposedly "developed" in this environment which they are told is professional; it feels as if there is more at stake than there generally is.

The bad language directed at game officials from coaches; the yelling and screaming at a young player because he made a bad pass or missed a tackle. Even giving a smack around the head to a player substituted, for in the coaches' opinion he made a mistake. If I had a son playing, that coach—and I use that title with reservations—would not be within a 100 miles of him. Punishing players with pushups or running laps around the ground if they lost a game. What a way to treat these young children, sending all the wrong messages to them, and not only potentially setting their professional development back but who knows what damage to their personal development?

US youth soccer has, in the last three decades, exploded. There are over five million youth players (two million of those are girls) registered in youth soccer with three governing soccer bodies: United States Youth Soccer Association (USYSA), American Youth Soccer Organization (AYSO), and Soccer Association for Youth (SAY). There are millions more playing in YMCA and recreational soccer programs. With such an increase in the number of young boys and girls wanting to play soccer new teams are being formed almost every week.

Groups of parents get together in order to start a team for their children and once agreed on a team name, number of players in the squad and which league to apply for membership the next questions is: who will be the coach?

Invariably, none of the fathers have played the game of soccer, let alone been a coach. But one or two of them will volunteer to take the role. Their next move is to the local library for a coaching book or soccer coaching video. Congratulations to them, for at the very least, they want to assist their children to improve their performances on the field.

The problem occurs as the new coaches gain some knowledge and then wish to play each player's game! The coach now wishes to shout instructions to each child every time they receive the ball. You now have a continuous stream of instructions from the coach to every player. As stated the majority of new coaches have never played soccer and too often the instruction or advice is incorrect. Let us not forget that the beauty of the sport is in its unpredictability and it shows the naivety of these fledgling coaches—who do have the right intentions—who believe they can dictate each passage of play. It is unlike the other popular American sports; a soccer coach does not have an important influence and contribution during a game as with time outs in other sports.

Now, add one more important problem. Most youth soccer leagues have rules that coaches and player benches are on one side of the field and all spectators, parents, friends must be on the opposite side of the field.

The scene is now you have a coach on one side of the field shouting instructions and a parent on the other side of the field also telling their child as to what action they should take. It's absolutely disastrous. Again, I repeat, in most cases neither parent or coach has played, or really knows, the game of soccer.

The player has invariably decided what action he or she is going to take as the ball approaches, all good players develop this skill, suddenly they now receive possibly two different instructions, one from the coach and one from the parent. The possibility now of three courses of action! Who does the child obey, their own decision or that of authority of the coach or their parent?

Indecision can now cause hesitation and may bring about the loss of the ball to the opposition. I have seen these situations over and over again and I feel for the children on the field. Please parents and coaches, let your children play and enjoy themselves. They do not need a continual stream of instructions from the sidelines on what to do. Let them make their mistakes, they will learn from them. Yes, coaches can send onto the player instructions perhaps for major points, marking a top opponent, moving back to defend or moving forward to support an attack but again, it's a limited amount of talk.

I do not know if parents and coaches behavior to their young player is bred from the actions in all other American sports? When you consider the amount of the coaches' control in American football, baseball and basketball where in football plays are sent from the coaches onto the quarterbacks who then relays them to the offense. In baseball, coaches signal to the batter what shot he should be making, or base coaches will be instructing the runner to stop or go ahead to the next base. The basketball coach signaling to the point guard the play to attempt or to taking a timeout to design a play for the players to perform. The coach in those sports is so in charge of his team and the plays to be made that do American fathers and coaches feel that they must do the same by shouting instructions to their children each and every play on the soccer field?

I remember my first game as coach of the Dallas Sidekicks in the Major Indoor Soccer League. We had selected a young player Eddie Radwanski, the number one pick in the US college draft, and Eddie was preparing to make his debut for the Sidekicks. As I instructed Eddie to prepare to come onto the field about ten minutes into the game he asked me what did I wish him to do? You can imagine my surprise; I can remember just shouting "Bloody well play!"

Eddie, having spent four years at University of North Carolina, may have experienced a system of receiving instructions similar to that which I described in US sports. Eddie developed into an excellent forward and was a member of the Dallas Sidekicks Major Indoor Championship Team in 1987 and played in the US National and Olympic team. Now a very successful University soccer coach, I know that he allows his young players to play and make their own decision as the game continues.

Jeff Banister, the manager of the American League baseball team, the Texas Rangers, stated the following when asked by a reporter, "Could you tell me everything I need to know about being a better sports dad?" "If you talk to your child while they are competing—even from a distance, even in a whisper—that's all they can hear. And it's the last thing they need to hear."

"When you are on the field as an athletic, especially as a young athletic, the people you do not want to disappoint the most are your parents," he says. "And when a child hears a parent's voice, especially one telling them what they've done incorrectly or need to do, it adds to the tension and the anxiety. When you're there and you're cheering and you're clapping and lending support, their feeling is so much greater. They're going to compete harder. They're going to focus. When they hear the clapping, they know they did something good. When my son started playing ball, I used to shout things from the stands. I used to think it was being helpful and supportive. That glower should have told me otherwise. Now I shut up during games. Don't say a word—just cheer and clap, that's it. And now the boy plays with a smile, even after a strikeout. I'm not his coach. I'm his dad. His cheerleader. His biggest fan." I shouldn't have needed Jeff Banister to remind me of that. But I'm glad he did.

That is great advice to all parents who have children playing sports.

Let children play and enjoy.

Coaches, do your work on the training field and let your players play in the game.

Parents, cheer and encourage your child or children.

If we can get those three areas correct, US Youth Soccer will be a far more enjoyable and entertaining experience for all involved and I am certain that it will better facilitate the development of tomorrow's soccer stars.

Of course, one important caveat is that we get the right coaches. Those who know the game.

It is crucial that we get this right within this generation because that will shape the long-term strength of the domestic game in the MLS. All of the provisions are in place but they have to make the best use of them. What we need to see is those young American stars coming through and the big money signings becoming less and less domineering.

That's not to say they shouldn't happen. They happen in every country in the world. And there can be significant benefits in certain examples. The transfer of David Beckham, who gave many years to the MLS and raised the profile of the league immeasurably, was wonderful from a marketing aspect. Unfortunately, it also had the side effect of encouraging an influx of, by comparison, mediocre players at far greater cost than necessary. Of course at that point there's the risk of going down the same road as the old NASL.

If it's a player who will be an asset to the league, like, hopefully, Kaka will be with Orlando if his injury problems are behind him, then the benefits make the cost worthwhile. It is a difficult position for Don Garber, the MLS commissioner to regulate such expenditure. Owners may be ambitious but certain rules like salary caps have to be maintained to retain a fairer and more level—and, crucially, stable—playing field. Toronto FC spring to mind as a club that has taken a few too many financial gambles that haven't paid off. They paid approximately £6m for Jermain Defoe and swapped him for Jozy Altidore who cost Sunderland £8.5m. Financially it was a deal that just about paid off but the truth is that it is a risk and MLS clubs are not in a position to regularly be spending money like the English Premier League clubs do. The last thing we need is the return of unscrupulous agents looking to exploit club owners who do not know much about the game.

In my humble opinion Commissioner Garber has done a good job and there are many areas in the game which I feel are strong. I think it is a positive move to enforce that new franchises must have a purpose built soccer stadium. It helps with pitch configurations for the game and also the supporter as well. The small and compact stadiums (with the exception of Seattle's larger arena) that have been built over the last few years have, by and large, been beautifully developed.

And although it's a fine line, Commissioner Garber has walked it carefully and I'm supportive of what he's done so far. Perhaps from time to time club owners should be reminded of their greater responsibility to the game and not get carried away with the possibility of short-term success that is unsustainable.

twenty

A New Life at Age 70

IN 1986, AFTER I'd been in Dallas for a couple of years, I was invited onto the board of directors of Dallas Cup, Inc. the international youth soccer tournament. I learned something of the inner workings and was present at the event itself but I quickly realized that my time constraints were so great with my commitments with the Sidekicks that I was unable to dedicate the appropriate time to the Dallas Cup. At the time, I wasn't only coaching the Sidekicks, but finding myself so preoccupied with the ownership problems that something had to give.

So I stepped away as a director and simply went to the Dallas Cup tournament as a spectator. As clubs from around the world participated, it presented the welcome opportunity to catch up with old friends from England.

When I retired as commissioner of the indoor league, I was in the process of finalizing my arrangements and handing everything over to the new commissioner when out of the blue I received a phone call from a board member of the Dallas Cup asking if I would meet her and another board member.

Those people were Judy Murphey and Ray Mackey, Dallas Cup board members. They informed me that their executive director had left and asked if I would like the role.

"Well, I'm retired," I said hesitantly. "I wouldn't want nine to five, five days a week."

"Oh no, that won't be a problem," was the reply.

They were right, it ended up being nine until nine, seven days a week!

I was in the role for twelve years. It was an incredible experience and a new lease on life at the grand old age of 70.

The Dallas Cup was founded in 1980 and had been a hugely popular tournament for young players but when I joined I discovered it was experiencing problems. Not so much with the organization or the work done by my predecessor, but, simply, the state of the world. This was immediately post 9/11 and so people were reticent to travel, let alone allow their children to fly internationally, and to America. There was a definite fear and many of the international teams had withdrawn. The tournament was no longer a top competition.

We received complaints because only American and Mexican teams were willing to compete, and subsequently, the sudden drop in popularity meant that financial problems had struck with immediacy. One of the board members had previously saved a prior tournament by securing some sponsorship funds at the last minute.

I was presented a difficult situation but I was also in a fortunate and privileged position because of my background. The first person I called to enquire about assistance was Sir Bobby Robson, then manager of Newcastle United. I explained my situation and without hesitancy he offered to send his coach Gordon Milne over with an Under-19 team. Just like that, I had a start.

I called on favors from friends like Bobby and before I knew it I had a few teams promised. And so, with that news, others were encouraged to participate too.

We had a small number of full-time staff in the Dallas Cup office; Randy Jones, the tournament manager, Sue Slater, secretary and volunteer coordinator, and Mary Link, Dallas Diversity organizer. We had no money to pay them in the summer months. I had to convince them that we'd be okay and fortunately, they weren't dependant on the money as they had spouses who worked. I reached out to Bill Nuttall, the president of sports equipment manufacturer Diadora. Bill, who I'd worked with during my time at the Sidekicks, immediately offered a four-year sponsorship for the tournament. I had equipment, and money, so I could pay the salaries of the staff who had worked so hard. It was a different kind of pressure to what I was used to, almost like a robbing Peter to pay Paul situation though no monies were robbed, I hasten to add!

At a board meeting after about three months, a couple of board members raised the suggestion of closing the competition down.

"How can you do that? I've only just come in!" I insisted. "Give me the time."

That word again.

There was an air of despondency. No one could see the light at the end of the tunnel. Making the Dallas Cup successful again did not happen overnight. For three years, the staff worked voluntarily through the summer months with the promise of later payment.

For that first year I felt that we needed something special to start to turn things around. Bobby Robson had been a huge help but I thought if we could attract Manchester United, the repercussions could be fantastic. I contacted Paul McGuinness, the assistant academy director, to see if they would bring over an Under-12's side. The club were receptive, but not to my request that the children would do a home stay (that is, to stay with local families who were helping as volunteers for the tournament). It wasn't part of their policy to permit that, so we had to find hotel rooms for them. It would prove to be a costly speculative exercise as the youngsters wouldn't be playing in any of the games that we would charge spectators for. I convinced the board that I would find the sponsorship money to make it worthwhile. I liaised with local hotels, asking them to provide rooms for international teams such as United with the promise that we would use them as a recommended partner for the American teams who would be paying for their own hotel rooms.

Once we announced that Manchester United were sending an Under-12 teams, we were inundated with requests and applications for teams in that age bracket What a breakthrough. When United came, people were lined up in their droves to watch them. They were a tremendous success and they came back the following year, too.

In 2005, when we moved into the FC Dallas stadium for the first time, we were able to persuade United to send over an Under-18 team. With our new arena in mind, I wanted to build anticipation early, so at the 2004 event we were able to announce that Manchester United would face Real Madrid in the opening fixture of the 2005 Dallas Cup.

It was a bit of a risk to ask them because only the winners qualify from the group to the semifinals and to put both of them in the same group meant we would lose one team early. When I explained this to both clubs, their response was the same. "It's your tournament." I felt that was terrific.

The publicity helps us attract a record crowd of over 17,000. It was a tremendous progression for us and helped us build on some great publicity in the 2004 tournament when we had the USA Under-18 side in the tournament. In their team at the time was a young player by the name of Freddy Adu, who was apparently fourteen. He had been given a $1 million endorsement contract by Nike and his presence at the Dallas Cup helped us achieve record financial results for the tournament, even greater than when Manchester United and Real Madrid came the following year, such was the interest in that young boy.

That spell resurrected the Dallas Cup from its lean period and almost instantly we became oversubscribed for participants again. That was great, because it enabled us to be in a position where we could put at least one overseas team in every group. And, of course, with Kansas City's young players defeating Manchester United in the first year, it gave the incentive and promise that our American teams could compete and come out victorious.

We made some amendments to the age brackets as we progressed through the years to refine the quality. Now I feel confident in speaking of the prestige of the Dallas Cup as one of the longest running international youth tournaments. Its success, is due to having good competition, good playing fields, top game officials and good organization. If all four are correct, you have a good tournament.

Before I go any further I do want to reserve special praise for the referees. The standard of refereeing is something I feel is of paramount importance and we always have top class referees at the tournament. It helps with the standard and also helps these younger players understand more about their own responsibilities and conduct.

There are almost two thousand volunteers who help out every year. A large number of these would be families whose children participated in the Dallas Cup, and so they might have provided a home stay for a visiting team. Many of these volunteers have helped for years and years. We have people who have been assisting us for three decades.

It's a real triumph of the community. The international teams will visit the local children's hospitals and schools to meet and greet with all the children. Over the years we have really embraced diversity and received worldwide publicity when we had a combined Israeli and Palestinian team and also a combined Catholic and Protestant team from Northern Ireland. The object being to demonstrate how sport can unite and witnessing the joy which has been brought to some of these children—many of whom know little to no English—has provided me with some of the most fulfilling moments of my life. We arrange for every team to fly their national flag at the tournament and of course, since there was no such one for the Israeli and Palestinian team, they informed us they would bring their peace flag showing the dove of peace. Their stay was a remarkably emotional one for everyone involved. Before they were due to leave, I was presented with one of their flags and it had been signed by all of the group, to "Gordon, a man of peace." I was so overcome with emotion I had to leave the room. Even writing about it brings the tears back to my eyes. We invited the Peace team again the following year because a Jordanian gentleman based in San Antonio offered to assist us in financing their return. Plus a local Jewish man also donated to make their visit possible. The impact of the Dallas Cup on the local community speaks for itself now.

I'm so very proud of my association with the tournament and I'm pleased that together with our staff and many volunteers we were able to improve the organization and the caliber of the teams involved. Basically, it is all down to contacts—and the old saying, "It is not what you know, it is who you know" was very true for us as we returned the Dallas Cup tournament to its prestigious place in international youth soccer tournaments.

NCAA college soccer is not the development ground for major league soccer players. With the continued expansion of teams in Major League Soccer one of the major questions asked is, "Where are the teams going to find the players of quality to fill their rosters?"

With roster restrictions on the number of foreign players allowed, teams must turn to home-grown talent. It has become increasing evident that the majority of NCAA college players are not going to provide this much-needed talent. With NCAA college soccer schedules providing on average only 20 games per season, it is far short of the number of competitive games required to produce "ready-made" players for Major League Soccer. Adding to this problem, the NCAA soccer substitution rules in which very few players are on the field for the full ninety minutes of a game presents a significant problem. How can a player, having a four-year playing career at college from an age of 18 until 22 years of age, gain the necessary experience needed for then joining a professional soccer club and being ready to contribute immediately?

If you compare the development of young soccer players in countries such as Brazil, Germany or England with that of a young American player, it is a difference clear as night and day.

The majority of young foreign players at professional clubs in their countries have been with those clubs while still at school, receiving coaching and in many cases playing in the clubs youth teams. On leaving school at 17 or 18 years of age and joining the clubs as a professional player they are then in fulltime training often with the clubs senior players and receiving coaching from the experienced professional soccer coaches, and playing in about 40 to 50 games per season.

The day-to-day competition to improve and become a member of the first or second team squad is fierce and starts the progress of becoming an experienced soccer professional at an early age. That period from 18 until 21 or 22 years of age is so vital in a player's development and one sees more and more players in that age group selected for top club's first teams around the world. With competition to be selected so high, many young professional players are released, even before they are 21 or 22 years of age.

Compare this "apprenticeship" to that of the young American player who leaves high school at 18 years and attends an American college. With a schedule of approximately 20 games with possibly only five or six of those games being really competitive, day-to-day training with a group of other young players and not having that competitive and higher grade of soccer that the Brazilian, German and English players experiences every day at their professional club. This playing/training schedule for four years leaves him way behind the foreign player in preparation for a professional career.

When I discussed this situation with college soccer coaches, they quite rightly tell me that their soccer programs are not in place to produce professional soccer players. They are there to provide a student athlete the opportunity to play his sport while he is provided with a higher education.

With the young American soccer player now more aware than ever of the world of soccer, and the opportunities to become a professional player abroad and in Major League Soccer, more players are leaving high school at the age of 18 and going abroad to join clubs or signing for an MLS Club and foregoing a college education; a highly debatable subject.

It is interesting to note that Jurgen Klinsmann, the former US Men's National Team Coach, had selected many young American players in that 19–22 age group from players playing overseas in European and Central American clubs. It is also interesting to note that there is at this time a plan being put forward to the NCAA sport governing body to restructure NCAA Division I Men's Soccer into a full-year sport.

The plan is to have two seasons, one beginning in September and one beginning in March with men's college cup finals in June. Will NCAA college presidents consider such a proposal? College soccer is a nonrevenue sport, unlike college American football and basketball programs which generate millions of dollars from their TV and sponsorship programs. To me it is interesting that many college athletes playing in the American football and basketball programs do not even complete their four-year programs. They are almost ready made for playing in the National Football and National Basketball teams upon leaving college. This is so unlike the college soccer player situation. One reason alone—finance. The monies generated in the NCAA football and basketball programs are in the millions of dollars and the participation of a college team in a Bowl Game or in the March Madness basketball tournaments often provides the financing to cover all the sports programs in a college. With so much money available to those sports programs, they are able to attract top caliber coaches to their colleges. So many former NFL and NBA coaches with experience of top level play in those sports are on the college coaching staffs so that the student athletes are receiving coaching at its highest level, thus making those drafted by the NFL and NBA teams to be well prepared for the demands of professional football and basketball. College soccer does not have that financial support to bring about a similar situation at this time.

There are changes that I feel are required to improve the standard of youth soccer and playing being developed, and I've already spoken of them, but one thing is true when observing those thoughts. They cannot be accomplished quickly.

That is not to say that in times of relative powerlessness, we sit back and do nothing. We should all endeavor to make the changes we feel we can achieve and so it was when I became involved with the Dallas Cup.

We were able to present a very unique experience for kids to compete against other children of all backgrounds, against some of the most esteemed soccer clubs in the world. We were able to do so in an organized, competitive fashion, but in a way that was also fun for the kids. It does provide a scouting opportunity for college coaches and foreign teams to see the best US talent.

We try and bridge the gap although what we cannot help is that youth soccer in the United States is an expensive pursuit. It can cost thousands of dollars in coaching fees, team fees, competition fees. I think it's the wrong thing to do because underprivileged children are missing out. I don't want to knock it unnecessarily but I feel there is a long way to go before it's right from an administrative point of view.

As I said earlier, I think, or at least hope, the change will come from the American players who have spent long periods of time overseas and noted how different the development process is for European clubs. They should be the pioneers for reforming in the North American game.

twenty-one

The Sleeping Giant

I WROTE ABOUT the aim of the US Federation to win the 2010 World Cup as was declared by the incoming president Doctor Robert Contiguglia in 1998. At the time, only seven different nations had won the tournament since its inception, so that gives an indication of how bold the statement or ambition was. All of the nations that had won it had years and years of running a strong domestic league. I can appreciate that Dr. Contiguglia got carried away and set such a lofty target with his enthusiasm. It was of course an unfair and unrealistic target.

Does that mean that their subsequent performances were disappointing, or failures? The United States is a relatively young soccer nation. They have qualified for the last eight consecutive World Cup Finals tournaments. In Japan in 2002 they reached the quarter finals. In 2010 they survived the "group of death" and put in encouraging performances in 2014. Is that not a success?

There was an article in *Soccer America* magazine in July 2014 by my very good friend of many years, Paul Gardner. He stated the following: "Thank you Jurgen and Goodbye" and "Time to move on from sterile Klinsman Interlude."

Basically, in his story, Paul was complimenting the performance of the US national team goalkeeper Tim Howard for his record number of saves, sixteen in a "World Cup" game between the United States and Belgium. But then, Paul quite rightly stated that in order for that statistic to occur, there had to be a record number of shots by the Belgium team. That stat invariably means that you're either not a very good team, or you're not playing well in the game. It should be remembered that the United States was not expected to win that game. The spirit they showed, even in defeat, drew a lot of admirers. Incidentally, it is games like that—with hopefully, in the future, the United States coming out on top—which will eventually change the perception of low-scoring games being classified as boring.

Paul compared the 2014 record of Jurgen Klinsmann with that of head coaches Bruce Arena, reaching the World Cup quarter finals in 2002 and Bob Bradley reaching the final 16 in 2010. In Paul's words: "Where is the progress?" And, later—he wrote "Under Klinsmann, the USA team has made no advance at all in either the caliber or style of its play."

Paul continued:

> "Klinsmann has led US Soccer astray. His insistences on ignoring young American talent while he brings in primarily German players with little or no connection with the USA has moved American soccer away from the much richer ethnic diversity that is the country's natural talent base . . . Klinsmann has comprehensively failed to deliver . . . Klinsmann should be dumped . . . The Klinsmann bandwagon is getting us nowhere."

That is strong criticism indeed, and Paul was not alone in belittling Jurgen. A number of the so-called experts on TV soccer programs have been quick to add their criticism especially the trend of bringing into the team a number of young players with US citizenship of the US servicemen fathers, who married European girls and settled in Europe. These young players are now playing in many of the second divisions of Germany, Norway and Sweden. This criticism of Klinsmann by the media possibly assisted in bringing forth his dismissal by the USSF.

We know that US college soccer is not the standard to produce young US soccer professionals at this time. Coming out of college at 21 and 22 years of age, having played 20 games a season for the past four years of their college soccer life has not developed them for top professional teams. This is very evident when one sees these players drafted into Major League Soccer and their performance when given the opportunity to play in the MLS teams.

Paul Gardner also stated in his article that Klinsmann was guilty of not giving young Hispanic players in the United States a fair shake. I firmly believe that the next US soccer star player will be a Hispanic player, but at present only a few Hispanic players are making their way into MLS teams. Fortunately we are seeing a number of young Hispanic players in the US National U15, U17 and U20 teams. It is just a question of time before we see their true potential. Funny, how we always return to "time," isn't it?

Time was Klinsmann's enemy but his decision to add these young players from Europe into the National team squad was again—in my opinion—the correct decision and "time" will prove him right.

The inclusion of such players as Bobby Woods of Ergz Ebige, Germany; Mix Diskerud, Rosenberg, Norway; Alejandro Bedoya, Nantes, France; John Brooks, Hertha Berlin, Germany; Timmy Chandler, Eintracht Frankfurt, Germany; Fabian Johnson, Borussia Moenchengladbach, Germany; Aron Johanasson, AZ Alkmaar, Holland; Danny Williams, Reading, England; along with the experienced players Tim Howard, Clint Dempsey (Seattle), Brad Guzan (Aston Villa), Brad Davis (Seattle), Michael Bradley (Toronto) and Kyle Beckerman (Salt Lake City) is a step in the right direction.

No one in the world would have forecast those two results against Holland and Germany in 2015. They were not lucky wins. They were well earned by excellent team play. Such a young side playing with confidence and style against two of the best national teams in Europe. The 2-1 victory over Germany, the number one team in the world, was particularly superb. Two exhibition wins does not mean that the US National team is now a "soccer powerhouse" but it does show that Jurgen Klinsmann's player development plan was on the right lines.

I have stated that US Soccer is a sleeping giant and it will be awakening in the not too distant future.

In spite of some of the stated problems for US Soccer at present, the standard of play in the US national teams at all levels has improved tremendously in recent years. With the program put in place by the USSF we are seeing a gradual all-around improvement in youth soccer throughout the country.

Major League Soccer is now in its 20th year with 20 teams at present—and two more cities to join in the next year—all with new soccer stadiums and, most importantly, they have youth team academies to assist in the development of young American players of the future.

Amongst all this talk of the future and the criticisms of some of the problems that still exist it is crucial that we appreciate how far US soccer has come in recent years. Can they win the World Cup in the immediate future? I would say no. But, to return to that sleeping giant analogy, it will not be too long before it does awake and a World Cup Championship is achieved.

twenty-two

Reminiscing

JOE MERCER, THE former Everton, Arsenal and England International midfielder and later manager of Manchester City, was a first class storyteller.

And for me, as the youngest football association staff coach in the sixties, I was always enthralled to listen to his stories at the coaching courses held each summer at the Lilleshall national football/soccer center. To many others Joe was a person who couldn't forget he was a former player and was an old man telling past stories.

I certainly didn't agree but I always felt that later in my life, I didn't want to be seen in the same light or manner. But it appears that in some instances I have become that "Old man telling stories." Too many friends have stated that I must write a book!

Two of the questions that I am most often asked is, firstly, "Who was the best player you coached?" and secondly "which was the best team that you coached?"

The answer to question two is easy, it was the 1972–75 Queens Park Rangers. So talented, winning promotion to the English First Division and one that finished second in the league in 1978 and played in the UEFA Cup in 1979.

Question number one is much more difficult. So many outstanding players and to name just one superior to all the others is for me impossible so I have decided to select my "Premier League Squad" of players that I coached. A squad with so much talent that would have been skillful, entertaining and so successful.

Goalkeepers:

Phil Parkes (Queens Park Rangers and England) A gentle giant. So quick and agile for such a big man and so commanding in the air. One of the best transfers in the Queens Park Rangers history, signed by manager Less Allen for £15,000 from Walsall FC, in the same week I joined Queens Park Rangers.

Carmelo Sedrun (Baltimore Bays and Spain) The "quiet man"—tall, slim and always in the right position to make a save.

Defenders:

George Cohen (Fulham FC and England) A member of the England World Cup winning team of 1966. A quick defender, sharp in the tackle and an excellent over-lapping full back. Always looking to join in the attack.

Frank McLintock (Arsenal, Queens Park Rangers and Scotland) "The Leader." A soccer brain. Always organizing the defense and always appeared to be in the correct position. Commanded respect of all the players as their leader.

Barry Kitchener (Millwall FC) Another gentle giant. Well over six feet. So commanding in the air and a strong forceful tackler. If you go to war, one of your first selections to be with you.

Dave Clement (Queens Park Rangers and England) "Mr. Reliable." A very talented skillful defender. Quick and joined the attack at every opportunity, an excellent passer of the ball.

Tony Hazel (Queens Park Rangers and Millwall FC) One of the most under-rated players in my career. A solid hard tackling player. Another quick player with a cannonball shot at free kicks.

Midfielders:

Bobby Robson (Fulham FC and England) A leader both on and off the field. Excellent technique and a great passer of the ball. Went on to become manager of the England National Team and manager of Fulham, Ipswich, Newcastle, Barcelona, and Porto.

Juan Santisteban (Baltimore Bays and Spain) A member of the magnificent Real Madrid team of the fifties and sixties, winning Spanish and European championships. A classic midfield, so skillful and a brilliant passer of the ball.

Gerry Francis (Queens Park Rangers and England) A player from the Queens Park Rangers youth team who progressed into the first team at 17 years of age. The "Complete Player." An industrious nonstop worker. Quick to move forward and score goals and also get back to defend. A major factor in the success of Queens Park Rangers in the seventies, and later, he managed Tottenham Hotspur.

Terry Venables (Queens Park Rangers, Chelsea, Tottenham, Hotspur, and England) The only player to play at every level of international football from youth to the England National team. Another excellent leader. Skillful with excellent technique. Another great passer of the ball. Quick to see that forward pass to his forwards. A great penalty taker. Life and soul of the team. Quick-witted and a typical "Londoner." An outstanding inventive coach.

Dennis Viollet (Baltimore Bays and England) One of the survivors of the Manchester United Munich air crash. A goal-scoring midfield player. So good in possession of the ball and cool and accurate in goal-scoring positions.

Forwards:

Allan Clarke (Fulham and England) Tall, highly skilled, center forward. Neat ball control and ice cool in front of the goal. Another first class penalty taker.

Don Givens (Queens Park Rangers and Republic of Ireland) One of the finest forwards I ever coached. The complete package. Fast, two-footed and skilled goal-scoring forward. Excellent in the air and first class ball control. Major player in the success of Queens Park Rangers.

Johnny Haynes (Fulham FC and England) Another leader. Excellent ball control. Superb passer of the ball and great goal scoring abilities.

Rodney Marsh (Queens Park Rangers, Manchester City, Fulham, Tampa Bay Rowdies and England) In the sixties he was the Queens Park Rangers' star. A very tall strong powerful goal-scoring forward. Tight ball control and very successful in one-on-one situations. Able to beat a man with exceptional ball dribbling skills.

Stan Bowles (Queens Park Rangers, Manchester City, Carlisle, Nottingham Forest, Brentford and England) An outstanding attacking forward. Tight ball control. Ability to beat a man and excellent goal-scoring forward.

Besides great individual abilities, he was a real team player. Worked hard with and without the ball. One of my favorite characters.

Dave Thomas (Burnley, Queens Park Rangers and England) A very fast attacking wing forward with excellent ball crossing ability. Setting up numerous goal scoring opportunities for his fellow forwards. Good at coming in from wing positions to score and always prepared to chase back into a defensive position.

John Seasman (Millwall, Luton Town) A very underrated forward. Excellent tight ball control and good passer of the ball. He was of slight build but great at holding the ball and working into goal scoring positions.

Oscar Fabbiani (Tampa Bay Rowdies, Palestino, Chile) A typical South American forward. Very skillful in possession. Able to dribble past opponents with great scoring ability. The perfect center forward.

That's a 20-man squad light on defenders, so I would add four solid hard-working players who served me as well, listed as follows:

Terry Mancini (Queens Park Rangers and Republic of Ireland) A wonderful character. Great team player who played to his strengths. Good in the air and a good tackling defender.

Terry Brisley (Millwall) Nonstop midfield player. Prepared to work up and back. Skillful on the ball and good passer of it. One of the first names you put on your team sheet.

Phil Walker (Millwall, Charlton Athletic) The perfect success story. A young player signed from a nonleague club at age 21 who developed into an outstanding midfield player. Very fast and good ball control always in support of his forwards and quick to see a goal-scoring opportunity for himself.

Mick McGuire (Tampa Bay Rowdies, Coventry City, Norwich City) A real team player, always giving 100 percent of himself. Good technique and excellent passer of the ball.

It's a tremendously talented and skilful group of players. Oh, to be able to have them all on one team. A joy to work with, good attitude, all prepared to work hard; and, I am pleased to say, all enjoyed successful football/soccer careers. My thanks to all of them.

twenty-three

Honors

IN DALLAS I have reached complete fulfillment in a professional sense. I have lived a long and fulfilled life, but it has been in Texas where I finally managed to reach the proper and truest contentment of a job well done. With the Sidekicks, I saw the position through until retirement from coaching and was able to pass it onto safe hands. With the Dallas Cup, I had an objective to restore the competition and elevate it to a greater profile and I can consider that was a job well done by the time I finally decided to retire from my position as executive director.

It was during my time—and, I believe, because of my time—with the Dallas Cup that I was given a number of great honors.

On October 11, 2006, as I approached the South Gate of Buckingham Palace with my wife June, daughter Kim, and her husband Donald, I thought back to the many times as a young boy that I had sat on my father's shoulders with my face pressed to the Palace railings as I watched the ceremonial "Changing of the Guards," in awe of the color, precision and splendor of the Grenadier Guards. Now, on this beautiful sunny October morning (not typical of English weather at that time of year) I was to cross the famed courtyard into the inner quadrangle, enter the Palace to meet Her Majesty, Queen Elizabeth II, and received the "Most Excellent Order of the British Empire."

The award had been made because of my work with the Dallas Cup. Michael Morley, who was the British consulate in Dallas, an ardent soccer and Chelsea Football Club supporter, felt that the efforts we had made to bring the youth of the world together should be recognized. I think he had been moved by the work we did with the peace teams.

Michael sent correspondence to the UK foreign office recommending an award of the "Member of the British Empire" for services to international youth football and that proved successful; in May 2006, Michael informed me that the award would be announced in London on June 1st. I would then be invited to meet the Queen at Buckingham Palace later that year to receive the award.

Upon entering the Palace, we walked past formally dressed courtiers and the Grenadier Guards in their splendid bright red dress uniforms. We climbed the impressive wide stairway, admired the beautiful paintings that adorned the Palace walls before being separated. I was led to a special gallery for the award recipients. A courtier accompanied June, Kim and Donald to their seats in the magnificent state ballroom to await the arrival of Her Majesty, Queen Elizabeth II. The orchestra of the Grenadier Guards entertained the 312 guests with a selection of music ranging from "The King and I" to "The March of the Cockleshell Heroes." The scene was set for the historic presentation of the Queen's Awards in the west wing of the Palace.

Meanwhile, members of the Queen's staff greeted us, the honorees, warmly. Our names and the award we were to receive were confirmed. In a splendid and elegant room, light refreshments were available, and I had the opportunity to meet and talk with many of the other recipients. I spoke with people from all walks of life—doctors, military, police and prison officers, Olympic athletes, representatives from the fashion industry, broadcasters and many more.

We were introduced to the Secretary of the Central Chancery of the Orders of Knighthood, Lieutenant Colonel Alexander Matheson of Matheson. He was an imposing man, well over six feet six inches in height; he welcomed us and congratulated us on our awards. He then explained the procedure for the presentation. He instructed us when we should go forward to the Queen, when to curtsy for the ladies and when to bow for the gentlemen, how to address the Queen (the first time as "Your Majesty" and anytime afterwards as "Ma'am"). We were now deemed suitably prepared and we could hear the orchestra play the opening bars of the national anthem—the signal that her Royal Highness was about to arrive in the state ballroom and the proceedings were set to commence.

We watched on one of four television screens in the gallery as the Queen entered the ballroom escorted by her entourage. Entering first was the Lord Chamberlain followed by two Gurkha Orderly Officers from Nepal (a tradition begun in 1876 by Queen Victoria). There were also five members of the Queen's bodyguard of the Yeoman of the Guard (an order created in 1485 by King Henry VII) and four gentlemen ushers to the Queen. History and tradition abounded in all aspects of the investiture.

We continued to watch the ceremony on the televisions as her Royal Highness received each recipient. The name and citation was announced as each honoree moved forward. The Queen entered into a brief conversation with each person and, as instructed during our briefing, when the Queen extended her right hand it was a signal that your time was up.

On this October day, 101 people received awards. Receiving their accolades during the 75 minute investiture were three Knights, one Dame, 11 Commanders of the British Empire, 28 Officers of the British Empire and 58 Members of the British Empire.

I waited patiently and eventually it was my turn to join a group of twenty to be escorted to the left side entrance of the state ballroom. For one final time we were checked by name and award—the organization and timing for the entire event was controlled superbly. I stood alongside a Navy Rear Admiral waiting to hear my name and citation "for services for the development of International Youth Football."

The time had arrived.

The announcement was made.

I walked forward and bowed before the Queen. She took the Order of the British Empire medal from one of her ushers and placed it on the clip that had been attached to my jacket lapel for this purpose prior to leaving the gallery in the west wing.

She welcomed me to Buckingham Palace.

"Are you still involved in the football program?" she enquired.

My old age must have been showing!

"Yes your Majesty," I replied. "I like to believe that this involvement was helping me to stay young!"

She laughed, offered her congratulations and wished me continued success. I shook her hand, backed away four paces, turned and "exited stage right."

I was then escorted to the rear of the state ballroom to watch as the final recipients received their awards. The ceremony ended with the repeat of the National Anthem and the Queen, escorted by her entourage, departed along the center aisle. I joined my family; naturally, they wished to see the MBE medal in its elegant presentation box. I do not mind admitting that at this time I was quite emotional and perhaps only then was I really aware of what had just taken place.

The ambience, the tradition, the history—the exquisite furniture and magnificent paintings contributing to the elegant décor of Buckingham Palace, the sense of pride that I felt and that I had actually met the Queen combined with the fact that I could share this wonderful occasion with my family began to sink in.

All that remained was the taking of photographs by the official Palace photographer after which we finally departed Buckingham Palace. At this time I realized it had indeed been a very special and memorable day.

Not bad for a kid who had grown up in the East End of London, survived the Blitz of World War II and became a professional soccer player.

I am very proud of my MBE award—to be nominated because of my own actions and accomplishments over a lifetime in "the beautiful game." My family and I will remember it with pride for the remainder of our lives.

We received a tape afterwards showing the proceedings. It included a voice-over from the Queen speaking about the award and why she felt it was important. I think I calculated that I had been 94th in line that day. Her Majesty had dedicated a real amount of time to each person and did not appear tired or frustrated when speaking to me. I already held her in the highest esteem beforehand but to witness her conduct and the dignified way she carried herself elevated that to an even greater plain.

I know that it was made possible by simply saying "yes" to Judy Murphey and Ray Mackey when they asked me to join the Dallas Cup as Executive Director. I had a wonderful twelve years in the role, and as well as the MBE, I was given the fine honor of being the first person elected to the "FC Dallas Walk of Fame."

In December 2010, I received a "Lifetime Achievement Award" at the ESPN complex in Walt Disney World. The person in charge at Disney, Patrick Dicks, was the son of the former Chelsea player and Bristol City manager Alan Dicks. Alan and I had played together way back at Dulwich Hamlet before either of us became professionals. I had been working with Patrick for a while regarding teams that were entering to play at a tournament at the ESPN facilities in Orlando before I found out he was Alan's son. I'm sure that Patrick had an influence in my being the recipient of the "Lifetime Achievement Award." It was made at the Christmas showcase event—and, that year, they had a high number of Dallas teams involved. It was almost like a home crowd when I received the award! It was very flattering to receive recognition for my dedication to the game in North America and it's only on such occasions that you take a proper look back and realize just how long you have spent. I had done it as a profession, not to be recognized, though to have this show of appreciation was most humbling.

In 2013, I was inducted into the US Indoor Soccer Hall of Fame. After 1984, indoor soccer was the only form of organized professional soccer in North America for many years. It was we who remained who had the responsibility for voting Alan Rothenburg as the United States Soccer Federation president who consequently helped re-establish the outdoor game.

As I turned 81 I felt that it was probably the right time to retire from the Dallas Cup and hand the reigns to younger blood. And, just as with the Sidekicks, I was able to hand over the responsibility to someone who I knew would be faithful to the work we were trying to do. Andy Swift had been a player in the Dallas Cup tournament when young and had acted as its media liaison officer volunteer for a number of years. Andy understands the heritage of the competition; it's in good hands.

Part of the objective I had in mind at the Dallas Cup was to present the opportunity for young American children to develop in a way that the rest of the world did. Now, obviously, we only had the children for a short period of one or two weeks but it was hoped that being around peers who were playing at professional clubs would be an experience they would benefit from. Subsequently, upon seeing the conduct of these professionals and how they treated their player's development, it was hoped that some of that would rub off on local coaches and parents. How long that message remained with them, I don't know, but considering the impact that the Dallas Cup has made then I would like to think that we have at least made a positive change or influence. I was able to take a wonderful self-satisfaction simply from the work we had done; to then receive the recognition from the Queen was a total surprise but the most incredible, too. I had enjoyed my work at the Dallas Cup; I hadn't done it for any purposes of self-gratification. If I could have accepted the award on behalf of all who worked at the Dallas Cup then I would have, but, at the same time, I am of course tremendously proud of its personal nature. I suppose if I'm honest then I do hold a special place for the MBE for a number of reasons. It was an award made outside of sport that recognized my contribution and although that was a contribution within the sport, it was essentially the societal aspect which was acknowledged. That had less to do with the sport itself and more to do with the values which I have held throughout my life—so it was affirmation and vindication that I was at least doing something right!

Meeting the Queen in 2006 wasn't the first time I'd been in the company of royalty. As a manager of a football club you receive invitations to various functions. The BBC Sports Personality of the Year, the Football Writer's dinner to name just two examples. You meet a lot of people, and receive further invitations. I had always been very cautious about the requests I accepted and advised my players to do the same. Sure, accepting an invitation to join a prestigious golf club may seem like an exciting event at the time but in no time at all they'll be asking if you can acquire FA Cup Final tickets for them. You have to sort the good invitations from the others and it isn't always easy; it was also advice I knew I had to take for myself, and so I turned down a great number of invitations to events.

At these events you would meet celebrities, and high-placed or high-powered business people. When we were at Charlton Athletic we were invited to see the making of a Bond movie, meeting 007, Sean Connery. My first brushes with royalty came at these functions, meeting Prince Philip and Prince Edward.

The invitations didn't end when we moved to the United States. I was invited to a function in Dallas and had the opportunity to meet President

George Bush Sr. Later, I attended a charity golf day for the St. Jude's Children's Hospital and had the opportunity to meet another President, Gerald Ford.

Within the sport itself there have been many great names I have felt fortunate enough to have conversed with. To have observed Sir Walter Winterbottom and Ron Greenwood at close quarters—and, also, to have played against Sir Stanley Matthews in his career and then attend a dinner with him in Toronto late in his life . . . these were all marvelous experiences of which I have strong, fond memories.

When I was starting out as a coach as still a young player, I was obviously unable to coach on a Saturday, so the Football Association gave me a role as an instructor for schoolteachers. They allocated a gentleman named Joe from the Central Council of Physical Recreation who would set up a school in Kent where we attended for six Monday nights. The Football Association would arrange for teachers to come to that school and I'd take the coaching sessions in the gymnasium. Joe would pick me up from my home in Blackheath and take me to the sessions. He had two sons, Michael, 14 and Christopher, 12. They would come and watch Charlton play so I'd give them tickets and meet them outside the dressing room on a match day.

Life went on, and I remained in contact with Joe and his wife, Eva. Sometime later, I was at a cocktail party at 6 Bedford Square, the headquarters of the CCPR and I overhead a lady saying "Isn't it terrible about Joe's son?" My ears pricked and I went over and asked what was the matter.

"You must have seen it, it's on the front pages of every newspaper!"

"No . . ."

"Mick Jagger, involved in drugs with Marianne Faithfull."

"Mick Jagger is Joe's son?" I was shocked.

I'd never put two and two together. I'd always known him as Michael so didn't pay attention to the stories as I might have done. Joe was the epitome of an English gentleman and I gathered he was a little concerned by all the media's account of Mick's conduct. I called Joe to talk to him and mentioned that I'd never actually realized that Michael (as he was to me) was "Mick Jagger."

A couple of days later, Eva called me to say that she'd spoken to Michael and he'd offered me tickets to go and see him perform at Earls Court. I was grateful but said I must speak with June; truthfully, the music wasn't to our taste, so we sent a message to say thank you very much, but we had to decline and we were sure someone else would appreciate the tickets more.

I kept in touch with Joe until he passed away at age 93. We'd send a Christmas newsletter every year.

It remains my best claim to fame that *I* gave tickets to Mick Jagger to see *me* perform.

twenty-four

A Life Fulfilled

WHAT A CAREER in soccer. Going back over records to put together these memoirs brings up some surprising facts and observations and it really makes me appreciate what a wonderful journey I've been on. I've been described as a pioneer before, and what a wonderful description to have, whether or not that is true in the eyes of others, I know that I have led the most unconventional path in the game. Nobody else can say they have managed in the top three divisions in England, the NASL, and the MISL, *and* managed the US national team. And to think, I was also considered so strongly enough for the England manager's position that I was interviewed. I find "pioneer" to be more of an explanation for ideas and innovations in the truest sense of the word. So, others may have their opinion on that matter, but I have walked a path that nobody else has. I always liked to be the first. Now, given the nature of how things have worked out, it's impossible for it to be followed. And it has been a most wonderful adventure.

Now, I'm retired but am still involved. There aren't many people who are fortunate enough to say that. And I do feel as if I am contributing, and enjoying. I work with the Dallas Cup, my association with them will never end. I also provide broadcasting play-by-play assistance with the Dallas Sidekicks although I try and only comment when I feel it is necessary. I don't think I've ever been one to waste words.

Upon retiring I had a few things to ponder. Had I always made the right choices? In a conversation with June I wondered what might have been if I'd taken the $72,000 that had been offered. These things happen so often in football that nobody may ever have known.

"Gordon, it's not you," June said. "You can pick up a phone and make a telephone to any football club in England and speak to almost anyone you want. That's because of the reputation you've built. You've lived right, you've done things right, and you haven't cheated anyone."

She was probably right. But I do feel fortunate. Fortunate, as opposed to lucky—I had the good fortune to be in the right place at the right time, or to make the right decisions. I don't consider that to be luck.

So many times I've heard people say something along the lines of "If only I'd done a little bit more" or "If only I'd tried harder." What a painful thing to have to live with. But then they only have themselves to blame.

I could do that. I could think of what may have been if I had not walked away from Queen's Park Rangers, the most enjoyable spell of my professional management career. If I'd have pushed more earnestly and confidently for the England job. But I consider my life to have been such a rich one *because* of the choices I have made. Perhaps it is easier for me because, by and large it has been my decision to say "when." The one exception has been at Tampa Bay, although June confided in me a long time afterwards that she had been so concerned about the pressure I was under that I suspect if it had gone on any longer she would have interjected. If one is to consider everything properly then we have to account for everything as it is and not just individual events. For instance, the Baltimore Bays role didn't end perfectly but that time changed my entire life. It shaped how I would approach management and presented me with a presence in the United States game. At the time it was a bad experience; in hindsight, it's one of the best things that ever happened to me.

I think of the time when it was written about me that I could have a career away from football. Maybe in part that was because I didn't spend all day every day obsessed with the game. I had plenty of interests outside of the sport.

I'd only been to two horse races in my life before I came to America—the Derby, as a guest of Jim Gregory, and to Royal Ascot, also as a guest.

In Dallas, I was invited to a lunch at the new Dallas racetrack with a trainer and one of the local sports commentators. A few of us from the Dallas Sidekicks were there, and a few from the Dallas Mavericks basketball club.

"Have you ever thought about owning a racehorse?" we were asked.

At that point I'd barely even thought about racehorses in my entire life! But six of us took the plunge and decided to put up $2,000 each for a horse. It came second in its first race in Louisiana . . . and then won its second race. The group grew from six to twenty-two and we had a whole series of successes. To date, we've won twenty-two races and subsequently won money, which was nice. It's also out of the ordinary, particularly for smaller groups like ours, to enjoy such success.

I'm not a gambler by any means, but I saw it as a great social event, mixing with jockeys and owners and having lunch on the day out. When you see your horse coming down that last straight, with a real chance of winning, there's a huge thrill.

I consider that I have lived a life fulfilled and maybe part of the reason for that is because I still maintain the enthusiasm and excitement for learning something new. I often travel to football clubs to speak to various people, and I love to watch training under the control of younger coaches and managers when I can.

I suppose I may have that natural predisposition to keep busy, and maybe some might expect that I would slow down in my 80s. But I've always like to keep active and, to be perfectly honest, it was having so many commitments that has helped to keep me going after June sadly passed away on December 8, 2014.

June Jago was a very strong person. Very wise, very well educated, and very strong. The manner in which she was able to express her views was wonderful, even in situations where her opinion may not be the commonly accepted one. It takes a special character to have the confidence to maintain their convictions in that sort of situation, and June was certainly that.

Her knowledge of sports and her life intelligence and instinct meant that her advice was advice I could trust. Not much got past her. She enjoyed the game so much that I'd take her if I had to go to a game to scout a player. I remember being told by the Tottenham assistant manager Eddie Baily, another very good friend, attending a game at Brentford, "You've brought your bloody wife again, you'll cause us all trouble!"

June and I had a magnificent 54 years together. More than a lifetime. When Kim came along, we made a great family. They were more like sisters than mother and daughter and, of course, it can be seen at length through the stories I have shared in this book that she was a wonderful wife. She was always forthright, honest and wise.

I would always say that I met June when she arrested me and gave me the choice of going to prison or marrying her. I would joke that I made the wrong choice as I'd have gotten out of jail years ago for good behavior! In the obituary I wrote for the newspaper I include that story and although our close friends understood, I heard that some were upset because they thought it was frivolous. I know June would have found it humorous.

I can laugh about those good times and strange times and I find comfort that even in those dark moments, we could find something to smile about. But it remains difficult. They say that time heals and that may be true but the pain remains fresh. I have deliberately kept busy assisting the Dallas Cup even in retirement. The board of directors wonderfully established the "June Jago Memorial Foundation" to raise money through the Dallas Cup. They asked Kim and myself where we would like the money raised to go and after a quick discussion we both agreed it should go to helping the families and children of Dallas police officers killed or seriously injured in the line of duty. It is already working and making a difference in its infancy. June remained involved with the police even in Dallas, attending functions and helping where possible, so we are delighted that her legacy will live on with the spirit she lived her life. It provides me with comfort to know that not only did she live a fulfilled life but the principles she stood for will ensure her name lives on making the profound contribution to society in the way she did when she was with us.

As a young boy I could never have anticipated or dreamed of the life I would go on to live. How much of that is down to chance? Some of it must be. It was chance, fortune that I lived through the Blitz to even tell the tale. The empty desk next to me as I went back to school. That could have been me.

I was too young to have emerged from that experience with a conscious desire to make the most of the days, months and years I did have remaining. But maybe the seed was planted as early as that; to work as hard as possible, and to live my life in a manner that was respectful to others but also in a way that ensured I made the most of it. A huge part of that was trying something different. That said, if someone had informed me when I was a youngster that all of these dreams would have come true, I could not have believed them. I have been fortunate that good things have come in my life from my principles and desire to enjoy life.

It is common that most embrace retirement and many can't wait for it but I have to confess that I have found the times where I have been able to contribute in some way to the improvement of young people's lives to be some of the most rewarding times of my entire life. And, in that respect, the fulfillment that I have received as a consequence has transcended something that can merely be described as an "enjoyment of profession," as I wrote earlier. It is an enrichment of life itself.

Afterword

YOU WOULD IMAGINE—and, rightly so—that most people in the sports world consider their achievements in life to be defined by what they accomplished in their chosen field.

Much rarer are those who choose to transcend those barriers and attempt to use that privileged profile to make a real difference in society. To do that at all deserves kudos but to do that in today's society speaks volumes about those individuals.

Gordon Jago is one such man. For one so conversational you are fortunate to hear him speak of himself in anecdotes or stories. He has been implored by friends and colleagues alike over the years to put his life experience down on paper and, at the ripe old age of 84 (eighty-two, when the process began), part of me believes it was only a semiretirement which was almost forced upon him that left him with the time to do it. His energy, enthusiasm and passion would put people half of his age to shame.

Like many whose list of life-achievements significantly predate the instantaneous, here-today, forgotten-tomorrow logging of the internet and social media, Gordon's primary concern (I'm sure he won't mind me saying this) was that his story wouldn't compel today's readers.

That is the humility of a man whose achievements include being arguably the greatest manager of not one, but two, of the proudest clubs in London, England. A man who left the second of those jobs on the grounds of dignity and principle and then rejoined the North American game where he then became arguably (and, I repeat the word *arguably* only because Gordon's modesty would insist I don't state absolutely) the most respected gentleman in the sport in that country, too.

Take for example, the story of the Dallas Cup with the Israeli Peace team. This story is told on these pages as something Gordon Jago simply did, but really, the profound impact it must have had on not only the visiting children but the host families is something that surely served as a humbling lesson in life. For contributions like these, Gordon was quite rightly acknowledged by the Queen.

I am happy—and, more than that, keen—to confirm what Gordon can't, or won't; he is one of life's genuinely good people, who has pioneered positive change within his sport and outside of it, too.

The process of working with someone on their life story is such that you inevitably grow close and on a personal note I can say it has been a pleasure and a privilege to know and work with Gordon; he feels like part of the family, but, even more than that, I wish to use the last words of this book to tell him that he is a true inspiration to me as a man and a human being.

Wayne Barton
January 2017